P9-DJA-477

CARRIERS OF THE SPIRIT

THE PASSIONATE PEOPLE

Also by Keith Miller and Bruce Larson

The Edge of Adventure: An Experiment in Faith
Living the Adventure: Faith and "Hidden" Difficulties

CARRIERS OF THE SPIRIT

THE PASSIONATE PEOPLE

KEITH MILLER & BRUCE LARSON

WORD BOOKS
PUBLISHER
WACO, TEXAS

THE PASSIONATE PEOPLE: CARRIERS OF THE SPIRIT
by Keith Miller and Bruce Larson

Copyright © 1979 by Word Incorporated, Waco, Texas 76703. All rights reserved.
No part of this book may be reproduced in any form, except for brief quotations in
reviews, without the written permission of the publisher.

ISBN 0–8499–2832–X
Library of Congress catalog card number: 78–65804
Printed in the United States of America

Scripture quotations marked NEB are from The New English Bible, © The Delegates
of The Oxford University Press and The Syndics of The Cambridge University Press,
1961, 1970, and are used by permission. Scripture quotations marked RSV are from
the Revised Standard Version of the Bible, copyrighted 1946 (renewed 1973), 1956
and © 1971 by the Division of Christian Education of the National Council of the
Churches of Christ in the U.S.A., and are used by permission.

Contents

Acknowledgments

We are thankful for the many people who have helped us directly and indirectly in the preparation and completion of this book.

Although Hazel Larson's name does not appear on the cover as an author, she has planned, rewritten and edited as one of us from the beginning.

To those who read all or parts of the manuscript in its rough form and gave us suggestions and constructive criticism we are especially grateful: Brooks Goldsmith, Carolyn Huffman, Greg Purnell, Gene Warr and Kristin Miller. We took some of their suggestions and some we did not, so we cannot blame them for any material left in the final draft which should have been deleted.

Because of sickness and heavy travel schedules all around we are particularly thankful for the team approach to helping us of our friends and editors at Word: Floyd Thatcher, Mary Ruth Howes and Pat Wienandt.

The publishers and authors of the works cited have been most gracious in granting us permission to use the quotations included here.

And finally we are grateful to Patty Smith and Loretta Germann who typed and retyped these pages so many times.

Bruce Larson
Keith Miller

For the Reader

by Keith Miller

This adventure with Jesus Christ has me so excited as I'm sitting here writing this that I can hardly contain myself. All my life I have wanted to have something to give people that would make their lives better. I have wanted to find some way that I and other people could live without the inevitable fears and tragedies of life crippling us and destroying the hope and the meaning of our existence. I have also dreamed of having something to tell people in trouble that would make a healing difference in their lives.

And I suppose beneath all these things I have secretly longed for a way to throw myself into God's arms like a child and to live with the kind of devotion I've seen in the lives of people like Paul, St. Francis, St. Teresa, Luther and Wesley. I've wanted to find a way in my own nondramatic circumstances in Waco, Texas, to discover what lies beyond conversion, witnessing, Bible reading, small groups, experiences like the baptism of the Holy Spirit, learning about basic honesty and love. When a person has experienced all these things and *then* feels restless, how can he or she find out what to do?

Lately these dreams and desires have been coming together for me. I am realizing in a different way how Jesus Christ has offered every person the kind of love, hope and personal sense of destiny the world is seeking so frantically. Alan Paton talks about why it was that Jesus, a religious figure, was able to capture ordinary people with what he said. "Why did Jesus hold spellbound those who listened to Him? It was because He showed them they were not helpless victims in the grip of fears, hates, the past, the world. They were the salt of the earth, the light of the world . . . something in them rose up to meet Him: they were caught up into the bondage which is perfect freedom: . . . in Him they found meaning for their lives, and there is no freedom like the freedom of finding meaning for

7

one's life, of becoming the instrument of a Lord who helps us to be what we were meant to be." And yet Paton goes on to say that in spite of the meaning, the message, the adventure, "many resist Him, believing that to follow Him is to lose the whole world."[1]

And I have always been one of these resisters, one who is so afraid to give up the familiar that I have a terrible time turning loose of the control even a little bit—however tenuous that control actually is—in order to let God take my life and use it in a way that would actually fulfill it for *me* as well as for him.

As a matter of fact, I have even resisted writing this book. I don't want to pay what I fear will be the price to love people the way Jesus does. And I'm afraid you're like me and won't want to read this for fear of feeling more guilty for not wanting to be God's passionate people, ready to live and die for Jesus Christ. I'm afraid I'll have to give up some of the things and relationships which give me security in the midst of the chaos of living today.

I also resist writing this book because I am going to try to tell the truth about what I see concerning us Christians. And I am afraid of your rejection. In many ways we in the average church are a boring travesty of the family of God. We talk about loving the world, but in fact we love neither the world nor each other. We often don't even take the time in our meetings to listen or to risk sharing our real lives. And in many of our attempts to help people outside our congregations we are almost bumbling incompetents. I have always been afraid to say these things and to deal with some of the outer and inner reasons they may be true. After all I wasn't willing to risk paying the price to try to develop better ways. But I am now.

In this book Bruce and I are not presenting a grand scheme for changing the world. We are going to talk about what it means to try to move beyond ourselves into the lives of other people and institutions in our own cities to produce change. How do we give and receive effective love and concrete help? Why do people resist being loved or helped? Why do we resist really committing ourselves to other people? And how can we go *far enough* to get beyond the fear of being involved and into a sense of gutsy adventure and happiness about finding our own destiny with Christ? We are convinced that we Christians are part of a game, a great game which we are to *enjoy* the process of playing—including taking our licks.

The plan of the book is to start with ourselves and the kinds of love and help we as individuals may be able to give and receive. We'll discuss the different reasons we may want to give and receive love and what happens when we do. Then we will move on to the problems that groups encounter when they want to help people, and finally to a look at what can be done to produce real and effective institutional and social change in the cities in which we live.

We believe that God calls each of us to different people and ministries. But he has been pushing back our horizons and we want to share some of the things we are seeing and hearing.

Besides the fact that Bruce and I think the loving and concrete helping of people is God's wish for his body the church, we have found that something about being involved with other people in creative ways is exciting and actually fun. When we have given ourselves to Christ as represented by our neighbor, we find that in some sense we are children again and feel at home in the world. We are in some way doing and being what we were made to do and be. We invite you to come with us on this adventure as we try to learn how to love our neighbors—and ourselves. It may be unsettling and scary to begin to commit this way. But we can promise you that it will not be boring.

Keith Miller
Waco, Texas

Chapter One

Called to Love

MEMORANDUM

TO: Bruce

FROM: Keith

RE: Chapter One—Called to Love

Dear Bruce,

In all the books you have written I don't remember reading about your own early experiences which led you to God—and to be called by him to love people in the relational way you've chosen. I think it would be great if you would begin by telling something about your own particular search for Jesus Christ and for love.

It's really fun starting this book with you. I don't know where its going to lead us, but I have this restless feeling I'll never be the same for our having written it.

Keith

The other day at a neighborhood party, I found myself looking across the room at one of our grown children who was engaged in an animated conversation with someone at least three times his age. An unexpected feeling of joy which was closely akin to love welled up in me. It occurred to me that at age twenty-five this young man has already fulfilled any hopes I might have had for his future.

Suppose, at some point in the past, he had asked me about my dreams for his destiny. Obviously, this is not a question that a child usually asks a parent. But just suppose. To be honest, neither fame nor fortune would have been high on my list of future hopes. Health? Possibly, but not at the top. There are better things. Most of all, I would want all three of my children to know that they are loved by God—and to love themselves for that same reason. I would want them to know the love and acceptance of a handful of good friends. I would want them to be involved in work for which they feel uniquely equipped and which they enjoy with or without the rewards of money and recognition. I would want them to be able to relate to neighbors and colleagues in such a way that others feel loved and of value in their presence. I would want them to know how to be authentic friends, lovers, and helpers.

I was still thinking about all this the next morning when it occurred to me that I had never asked God what his dream was for me. Since my conversion many years ago I think I have felt, not always consciously, that I should be "doing great things for God." I have assumed he expected me to be a high achiever, helping people and "doing good." Surely the Christian is called to give his all to build his master's kingdom.*

But in the midst of all this ruminating, suddenly I remembered something Keith had said in a recent phone call—that people are

---

* We are very conscious of the many injustices done to women over the years and think it presumptuous that many male writers have referred to all persons as "he." In order to avoid the awkwardness and stylistic difficulties in always using both masculine and feminine pronouns, we will often use "he" in the traditional way. But we will mean *both* men and women unless it is obvious by the context that we mean only men.

always reluctant to be cannon fodder in someone else's war. Cannon fodder! Certainly, this is not what I want my children to be. I don't want them to lose their uniqueness, their identity, fulfilling other people's dreams for them. I want them to become all they can and to blossom and to find everything God has for them.

But if I, being evil, want this for my children, how much more must the Lord himself want the same for me . . . and for all of us in his creation. His dream for us goes far beyond service and achievements. And this is, in part, what this book is about. It is about serving and helping and sacrificial living as we are commanded by the Lord—but with the realization that in the process we can become all that we are meant to be.

All that we are meant to be! God's dream for each of us is so vastly greater than the largest dream we have for ourselves. But what is his dream for us? I believe he has given us clues to what that dream is. And the longings and yearnings buried in each of us often provide those clues. It is like being on a cosmic treasure hunt. Follow one clue and it will lead you to another . . . and then to another . . . until you find the treasure himself. For to find God and his ultimate will for us is to find ourselves. This is the discovery for which all of creation stands on tiptoe—to see God's sons and daughters coming into their own.

My own personal treasure hunt began as far back as I can remember. One of my first "clues" was an overriding feeling of loneliness. As a matter of fact this feeling is one of my earliest memories. My awareness of loneliness took a different shape in every phase of my growing up. But it was always there. When I was very young I dreamed often that my parents had died, leaving me all alone. You see, they were my only family. I was the solitary child of a couple who were old when I was born. My father was sixty and my mother was forty. They had separately immigrated from Sweden and met and married in Chicago. In both cases, they were the only members of the family to come to America. So I had no grandparents, no uncles or aunts, no brothers or sisters. If my parents died, I would truly be all alone. I can still remember all the details of the recurring nightmare in which I attended their joint funeral . . . and was left all alone in the world.

When I was four the stock market crashed. From that day until the day he died, my father's business was in grave financial difficulty. The sheriff was always lurking in the shadows about to put a padlock on a bankrupt laundry. The practical implications of this were that we moved literally every two years, looking for cheaper housing. All through my growing up years I was the new boy in the neighborhood—the last one chosen for sandlot ball and the first dropped from the guest list of birthday parties when the list was getting too big. All through those lonely years I can remember wanting more than anything to belong to a gang—my gang. I didn't even want to be the leader of the gang—just an indispensable member of it.

On my thirteenth birthday we had just moved to a new town. We were living in two rooms of a rundown apartment hotel. My mother planned the party and cooked my favorite meal, roast pork stuffed with prunes and apples (a Swedish specialty) and invited about a dozen people—none of whom were under seventy. So began my teenage years.

Then the shape of loneliness took on romantic overtones. I was in love with love and desperately wished I had some girl who cared about me. I have indelible memories of sitting in my room doing homework by the open window on the first warm days of spring. They were unbelievably bright after a harsh Illinois winter. The warm winds rustled the forsythia bushes and made the lilac buds nod. I pictured what it might be like to walk down the street in the springtime holding some special girl's hand. My yearning for someone to love who would love me was experienced as a great weight.

I guess I was not very negotiable, because the girls I wanted never wanted me. By the time I was in high school we had moved to an affluent Chicago suburb. The trouble was that we lived in the low-rent district. My clothes were usually too small and not very sharp to begin with. The family car was old—no competition for my friends' classy new models. And, what was worse, I had never learned to jitterbug. In those days only social lepers couldn't dance the "Lindy." No wonder my stock was low.

While I was in high school, America entered World War II. I proudly served as a junior air raid warden and an assistant block captain. I enthusiastically bought War Bonds. By that time I was earning my own money with after-school jobs and summer employment picking crops or working in the oil fields. One season I managed the lunch counter at the local Walgreen's and brought home the impressive salary of $18 a week.

As the war continued, propaganda films proliferated and my own sense of outrage grew. Most of all I wanted to do something about the destruction of millions of Jews. At seventeen, in a burst of patriotism and against the wishes and advice of parents and friends, I enlisted in the Army.

Although I didn't see it at the time, the connection between the lonely boy who so much wanted to belong and the impetuous idealist who wanted to do something about wars and atrocities seems obvious now. Since I have become a Christian, I understand that God had placed in me, as I think he does in all of us, in varying degrees, a deep hunger to belong and a great desire to help people who cannot help themselves. These were two clues in my personal treasure hunt of life.

My disillusionment with the Army lifestyle was instantaneous and almost total. But one of the great serendipities for me was finding a family. Without knowing it, I had been looking for many years for the Fourth Platoon of I Company, 397th Infantry Regiment. Those thirty men who trained together and ultimately went overseas to fight in France and Germany became a caring, fighting, drinking, singing, lending, griping family. We alternately loved and hated each other—just like a real family. As much as I despised Army life, I felt that in some strange way I had come home.

While we were still training at Fort Bragg, North Carolina, my father had surgery. The Red Cross arranged an emergency furlough and I sat up all night on a dirty train as it clanked through the Midwest to Chicago, desperately hoping that my father would not die. I arrived with the dawn only to learn that he had died a few hours before. I think I wept without interruption for twenty-four hours. And, though I loved my father, my tears were not for him, but for my own loneliness at losing him.

On the day before the funeral, an enormous box of roses arrived with a card that said "Our love and sympathy. The Fourth Platoon." In that moment the biblical phrase "The Lord giveth and the Lord taketh away" was especially applicable. In this case, the Lord had taken away my dad—and had given me—*family!*

It was a whole year before my old nemesis—"loneliness"—caught up with me again, and I will never forget that awful night. It was during the last winter of the war. Our division was on the line, fighting in the Vosges mountains in Alsace-Lorraine, an area between France and Germany proper. Due to some tactical error, our company managed to move ahead of the rest of the regiment and nightfall found us on a wooded hillside without food or blankets, surrounded by the enemy. The plan was to dig in, spend the night and try and fight our way back to friendly lines at dawn.

The enemy had other plans. They knew and understood our position. We were the proverbial fish in the barrel and they commenced to shoot at us with timed-fire artillery. Shells exploded in the air and released great showers of shrapnel into open foxholes. It was a terrifying, eerie night, full of manmade lightning and thunder. Branches of trees rained down upon us with each shell burst.

I was sharing a foxhole with a new replacement named Riley who had been assigned to my squad just the day before. Sometime past midnight a large piece of shrapnel found its mark in Riley's midsection. I tried to treat him with our two first-aid kits but there was too little for too much. I crawled over to a neighboring hole to fetch our company medic but it did not take him long to see that Riley was beyond his skills. We'd need to get him to the battalion aid station if he was to have a chance of making it. The medic administered a shot of morphine and went back to his own foxhole.

As a squad leader, I was responsible for getting Riley back to the aid station. I spent most of that night crawling from foxhole to foxhole looking for a volunteer to help me carry the litter. No one had ever heard of Riley. And no one would volunteer. Through my anger, tears and fear, I had to admit that I wouldn't have volunteered either had it not been my responsibility or one of my best friends. I crawled back to the foxhole, held Riley in my arms and felt him die with the coming of dawn.

I never felt so alone in my life. I sobbed for Riley and for his wife and children whose pictures he had proudly displayed the day before. But I knew somehow that my tears were also for my father and his death and the loneliness I still felt. Perhaps most of all I sobbed for me and my fresh awareness that when the chips were down, I would probably be as alone and friendless as Riley had been. My dream of a caring family—of belonging—was shattered. In the cold light of that dawn I grew up. I became a "man" in one night, which is to say that I became a cynic. I had come full circle. The lonely little boy had become a lonely grown man—who would "never trust anyone again."

Months passed. The war ended. Occupation began, and with it dullness, boredom and moral stagnation. I felt that I was swimming in a sea of garbage. Even worse, the garbage was inside of me. But that was evidently the prologue for God's next act in my life.

For God had a witness in our midst all through the years of training, fighting, and occupation. He was our regimental chaplain. He was anything but relational and did not make friends easily.

He was sober, serious, and sincere and wore his Victorian morality like an unyielding suit of shining armor. He publicly denounced the things he saw most of us doing every day. He was not someone you would easily confide in and probably the last person with whom you'd choose to be marooned on a desert island. But (and I will never cease to be thankful for that "but") he was a man who had a personal relationship with Jesus Christ and spoke about it convincingly. And as unattractive as I felt him to be, this man's faith did make him different in a positive way from the rest of us. Many of us were church members who believed that someone called Jesus Christ had died for our sins. But the chaplain was someone who had a day-by-day relationship with him. And because of that one life in our midst, God showed me during those months that there are two very different ways to live—for and by yourself or for and with him.

One night I was standing guard in a bombed-out building on the hills surrounding Stuttgart. I was fed up with myself and ashamed that I had taken on the coloration of the social and moral garbage of my surroundings. More than that, I began to sense that the dream each of us shared, to return home to normalcy, was, in fact, nothing but a dream. Returning to loved ones, jobs, careers, schools would not really change us. What I was now in Stuttgart I would always be, unless I opted for the alternative I saw before me. My overseas environment had not made me what I was. It simply revealed what I always had been and always would be. There was no veneer. The future was uncertain. But clearly the choice was mine.

I took my carbine off my shoulder and laid it against a brick wall, ground out my cigarette, kneeled down and looked up at the stars in the night sky through the charred rafters of the building. I prayed my first real prayer. "Lord, if you really are there, and, if you really do love me and want me, please come in and take over my life."

During the days and weeks which followed, quiet miracles took place—of morality and cleansing, of changed values and goals. I seemed to have new eyes to see and new ears to hear. But at first I told no one, for fear that I was on a trip that wasn't genuine or would not last. But it was real and it did last and has continued to this very day. That is not to say that there are not days when the whole adventure of faith does not seem unreal—or when for my own convenience I wish it were all a lie. But the relationship to

Jesus Christ that I saw in one hardshell Baptist infantry chaplain has become the central reality of my life.

Eventually the Army sent me home. And Chicago seemed very different. In those early months as a new civilian I can remember vividly walking the streets in the Loop and on the near Northside and feeling a great sense of love for every person who walked beside me or crossed my path. I felt as if I knew the ultimate secret about life—that God loves us and cares about us and has forgiven us—that Jesus Christ wants to live in us and with us and share our lives.

I can remember feeling very special because of this secret. It was as if a shaft of powerful light followed me wherever I went. I was both delighted and embarrassed by this sensation of walking in a shaft of light. As self-centered as it seemed, it was nonetheless real and powerful. Years later I discovered that Hannah Whitall Smith in her classic book *The Christian's Secret of a Happy Life* had a very similar experience.

As I walked the streets I looked strangers in the eye and ached for them to know and share the secret. I must have prayed silently for hundreds of people each week on my walks along Chicago streets. I would have given anything just to help one of them find God. No longer lonely, I yearned to help others find a way out of their loneliness. I wanted them to be able to walk in a dark world at the center of an unquenchable shaft of warm light. I wanted to help people with all my heart.

A lot of years have gone by since that passionate and single-minded young man walked the streets of Chicago. And, though much has happened since, some of which has made both the believing and going seem very difficult, the passion has never died. I believe that many of us who have had this experience of being saved from loneliness are captured somehow by a deep concern for others and a desire to help. This book is dedicated to those others who have been captured by this concern from God and don't know where or how to respond to it in loving others.

Keith and I are trying to discover how to become effective in helping people and how to be a leaven in changing the social and physical worlds we live in. We are trying to find out about being salt and light and leaven in concrete ways. This book is about learning to love by feeding the hungry, helping the people who are crippled by the depersonalized institutions and forces of contemporary life.

And we believe that with the help of the Holy Spirit we *can* begin to do those things in ways which will have real meaning for everyone concerned.

But basically this is a book for Christians who are filled with longings and vague unrest, seeking more of the Lord and not knowing where to look. We believe that for those of us who have begun with Christ and cannot turn back, spiritual growth and personal fulfillment lie buried in our neighbor's pain. Help him and we help ourselves. Take his silent cry seriously and we may walk out of our own prison. It is a paradox. We lose to find. It is the unconscious path to wholeness.

Freezing to death, I am told, becomes very easy near the end. A sign that you are near the end is the false feeling of warmth, drowsiness and comfort. To trust that feeling is to die. Faithful companions will force you to action, however painful, to save your life.

This book is aimed at bringing together people who want to be prodded into life-saving action by helping each other walk the adventure of faith to the very end, whatever the cost. Along the way we may do some good and lift some burdens and change life for those around us. But, whether or not, we together will begin to become the dream that God has had for us from before our conception.

T. S. Eliot once wrote that every person has basically two choices in life.

> We only live, only suspire,
> Consumed by either fire or fire.[1]

Most of us know only too well that hell, however you comprehend it, is fueled by the fires of hate, jealousy, indifference, indulgence, greed, selfishness or smugness. The other choice is the life Jesus calls us to, and it is also fire, or passion. He, in his passion, has loved us totally, withholding nothing, suffering everything. When we respond to his passion he calls us to become lovers by his Spirit. "Love one another as I have loved you." In every century, bands of his followers have understood this and have become the passionate people of God. They are filled with the other, the creative kind of fire . . . the fire of love.

MEMORANDUM

TO: Keith

FROM: Bruce

RE: Chapter One—Called to Love

Dear Keith,

I was thinking today as I started this first chapter of our book that it has been five years since our first book and study course, **The Edge of Adventure,** was published.

It seems to me that this kind of book—on being and doing God's work in the world—is the natural offspring of that original course, designed to introduce people to the whole adventure of faith in God.

I'm glad we settled on our title—**The Passionate People.** To me, you are someone who embodies the kind of passion we're trying to talk about—someone who cares deeply about people and about God's causes in the world. Why don't you begin your part of Chapter One by telling our readers how you got that way?

God be with you!

Bruce

The past three years have been the hardest of my life. At times I have ached with loneliness, frustration, fear, intense anxiety, deep hostility, cringed at the fear of rejection, sat alone with rejection itself—almost despair. There were days when I didn't know if I'd make it. No matter where I looked I felt like a misfit and wondered if I'd ever be happy again. At one point I cried out to God in my misery: "Am I the only one who can't get it together? Are all other Christians able to pray and read the Bible and have their bruised and broken relationships healed? Or are there out there someplace other men and women committed to Christ, yet amazed and crushed by their own sin and that of others and their inability to make things right for those around them? Is there a way to find hope and happiness, for us Christians who've failed and have to begin again?"

My part of this book will tell something about what I have been learning from the cauldron of my own pain and failure and how God seems to be using these things as a way to move me into a different and seemingly more honest and passionate involvement with people—a different way to respond to God's call with my life.

Years ago, when I first tried to make a serious and specific commitment to God, Christianity seemed relatively simple (as I look back). Since I had never believed in conversion experiences, I had trouble knowing what to think when I was confronted alone one day in a car beside the highway near Marshall, Texas. And although I have told some of you about this experience in *The Taste of New Wine,* I must include a brief sketch of it here so that you can see the lens through which I am looking at the call of God to love.

I was going through a tough period in my twenties which included frustration about my identity and vocational future. I'd finally come to the end of my rope and was so disturbed I was afraid I was going to have a nervous breakdown. One hot August afternoon it got so bad that I checked out a car from the oil company I worked for and started driving eastward from Tyler, Texas, as fast as I could. Irrationally, I felt that time was running out somehow and, worse, I had run out of hope—so I had to get away. As the tall pine trees flickered by on either side of the road my mind was a

22

kaleidoscope of scenes from the past. My palms were sweating. But then, in the midst of my flight, I pulled over to the side of the highway because I realized that even if I ran forever, there was no way I could run away from myself. And when I stopped, I added, "Or from you, God."

As I sat there in near despair, I began to weep like a frightened little boy, which I suddenly realized I was inside. I looked up at the clear August sky. There was nothing I wanted to do with my life. And I said, "God, if there's anything you want in this stinking soul, take it!"

There wasn't any ringing of bells, flashing of lights or visions. Instead I realized that God didn't care about all the performing I'd done all my life to win love and acceptance. I realized that he had been waiting for my "permission" so he could come into my life and show me who he is, who I was designed to be, and how to live. And there at the end of my rope I had given him that permission.

As I sat by the road I continued to cry, only now the tears were a release from a lifetime of being bound by myself, by the terrific drive to prove I am something—*what* I'd never quite understood. But whatever I had been, I felt accepted that day. And in the months which followed, I began to feel that I had never really grasped the meaning of being alive, growing and relating to people.

It was as if God had issued me a new set of eyes. I saw persons and truths underneath the "appearances of reality" around me. Behind sophisticated faces and Brooks Brothers suits I saw small boys still trying to prove to a daddy that they were OK—when some of them had already succeeded past most men's dreams. Behind the makeup and designer clothes of beautiful women of all ages I saw scared young girls who were afraid they were losing their beauty or were unloved, or who felt life slipping by and they'd never done anything but nurture children and wonder whatever happened to the dream of the sensitive and affectionate white knight they thought they were marrying. I saw people everywhere looking for the meaning of their own lives.

For four years I didn't tell anyone what had happened to me, but I prayed and read the Bible and the lives and works of the church's saints. But after the initial burst of passion for God and people—the honeymoon period—subsided, I realized that I felt very much alone on the Christian pilgrimage, even though I was teaching the Bible at church and had begun to witness. I had never liked to meet with small groups. I've always been a loner. But as I read the Bible and talked to more mature Christians I realized that it is dumb (and isn't even Christian) to try to go it alone. Besides, although I hated to admit it to myself, I needed to find some balance and some people to understand me. So out of my own need, and with great fear, I started my first small group.

At first we were a little guarded and formal as we prayed and studied, not revealing much of ourselves. But finally one night in a circle of caring eyes I tried to confess who I really am behind all my talking. It was terrifying, but they didn't run away. And we began to be able to weep over our own mistakes and sins (and those of others) and to try to make restitution where we could and begin again. We started timidly to be able to tell our hopes and dreams— and the happy feelings we had about just being alive and a part of God's people. To my amazement, as we went through the process of confessing and sharing, we felt accepted and ministered to by each other. And I began to experience the passionate love for God and people again.

During my four years "alone" when I had begun to wonder what God might want me to do with my life as a Christian, I'd thought, "Man, I'd love to figure out how to tell the lonely, hiding men and women in my generation about the hope and sense of being loved that I'm finding on this adventure with God!" I wanted to go tell them all!

And the Christians I'd gotten in with told me that this witnessing verbally was the most important thing to do. They pointed out that this was the "great commission" Jesus gave his disciples as he was leaving them:

> Full authority in heaven and earth has been committed to me. *Go forth therefore and make all nations my disciples;* baptize men everywhere in the name of the Father and Son and Holy Spirit. . . . And be assured, I am with you always, to the end of time (Matt. 28:19,20, NEB).

So I'd set out to tell people everywhere I could that there is hope in Christ and a new way to live for him.

But then, several years later, in a small group of adventurers redis- covering God's love and acceptance—I saw that answering the Great Commission to make disciples by leading them to Christ was not enough. People can make a verbal Christian commitment without either becoming disciples or loving anyone. And God seems to have a purpose for us *after* we meet Christ. I saw that purpose to be that we can learn to give and receive the same love which came to us in Christ. And that the giving and receiving of that kind of love is the mark of a true disciple:

> I give you a new commandment: love one another; as I have loved you so you are to love one another. If there is this love among you, then all will know that you are my disciples (John 13:34,35).

For almost twenty years I lived in a whirlwind of witnessing, small groups, conferences, prayer, Bible reading, studying and writing. I knew we were to witness and make disciples and to help people learn to give and receive love.

But something began to happen about five years ago that is adding a whole new color to the gospel for me, and to the picture of what it means to be God's passionate people. Almost at the midlife marker, after twenty-five years of being married, I began to feel quakings and rumblings in the foundations of our home—when the kids were leaving the nest. I spent three years in counseling, prayer, getting in touch with feelings of hostility and love I'd repressed all my life . . . and running from God.

My whole life seemed to crack open. I was afraid to face myself and yet knew I had to then or perhaps I never would. It was a frightening and terribly painful time.

As I read the Scriptures through the lens of my own pain and sense of having lost touch with God, I saw many things I'd never seen before. For one thing, I saw with new clarity that I have studied honesty so much because of my own fear of it—because I am afraid of failure and of being known and rejected. And I was even more afraid to find out the source of the enormous energy and anxiety that I had hidden from myself, like a great black beachball I'd pushed out of sight in my unconscious.

But I also learned something else, as I came back to Christ and read the Scriptures—something which had been there all along but which I hadn't been ready to see before: the God of the Bible is not primarily interested in our "evangelism" programs or in our "small groups" or even in our "piety." He's evidently not really even very interested in religion. But he is passionately interested in people, people in pain—all kinds of pain, things like hunger, cold, sickness, and poverty—as well as in our experiences of sin, anxiety, and lostness! As a matter of fact, Jesus said that he was going to be so immersed in people's pain and hunger and loneliness that we will meet him personally as we contact the hungry, thirsty, or sick person (Matt. 25:35–36). If that's true, then witnessing and small groups are important only as God can use them as doorways through which he and we can come to meet the people and heal the pain and separation *in the world!*

And I began to see that the concrete helping of people where they live is the sacrament—the outward and visible sign—of the passionate love of Jesus I have been hoarding in my own heart. The call I had felt to love him had led me at last to consider meeting him, where he works, in the pain of other people.

Chapter Two

How Come It's So Complicated?

MEMORANDUM

TO: Bruce

FROM: Keith

RE: Chapter Two—How Come It's So Complicated?

Dear Bruce,

Before we talk about helping in our churches and communities, I think we ought to discuss how it feels to love or be loved as persons. Recently I've found that helping and especially receiving help can be difficult and painful and can complicate and harm relationships if one is not aware of the various resistances involved and that there are different styles for being a loving helper.

Why don't you begin by describing the day last year when you almost got killed and how that started your thinking about the whole question of giving and receiving love as a Christian?

If you'll keep sending your originals of each chapter here, I'll put them together with mine as we go along.

The trees are bare now. Autumn is really over. There is a good feeling about this somehow. As I was jogging this morning, it occurred to me that God sort of cleans house every winter to get ready for a new spring. The processes of nature seem a lot less complicated than those involved in loving people.

Keith

One day this past summer I almost drowned. I had taken our daughter Christine and her friend Maria shelling on a small island in the Gulf of Mexico off our Florida coast. It was a calm afternoon when we landed and the three of us wandered up and down the beach intent on locating as many fine and rare shells as we could. I was almost totally at peace as I searched the water around my feet for special king's crown specimens. Suddenly I felt the wind change and in just a few moments, it seemed, the full fury of a tropical storm slammed against the island. As I looked at the angry turbulence of the clouds, my stomach tightened. We ran back toward the curve in the beach where I had anchored the boat only to find that it had drifted out about a hundred feet from shore, dragging its anchor. Evidently I hadn't let out enough line for the anchor when we had landed. We were stranded on a deserted island. I looked at the black convoluting sky.

In desperation I plunged into the surf and swam toward the pitching boat. In just a few moments I was getting very tired and I realized that the wind was driving the boat farther out away from the shore much faster than I could swim. Suddenly alarmed, I decided to swim back. But when I turned back and tried to head for shore, the tide, the wind and the waves were all against me. By then I could hardly see through the sheets of driving rain. Now a real alarm went off in my chest and I had trouble getting my breath. No matter how hard I tried it was impossible to make it back to the little island.

Then came an engulfing wave of fear and panic, but I did two sensible things. I took off my sneakers and I prayed. I remember gasping to God and telling him that if this was the end I was grateful for the whole adventure of life to date and was eager to see what came next. But then came a bizarre and practical thought, one which prompted me to complain to God about his timing. I had just invested several thousands of dollars in dental bridgework—money my wife was certainly going to need to bury me. I shook my head and smiled in spite of myself just as I realized I was not going under.

I stopped fighting the wind and waves and concentrated on keeping afloat. After a time I began to feel a sense of assurance that calmed my panic. The water was warm. If I could stay afloat in a swimming pool for hours why not in the Gulf of Mexico? And as panic left, strength came, and I found it comparatively easy to stay afloat even in huge waves, high winds, and a blinding rain. Possibly I had a chance after all.

About an hour and a half after I had made peace with the fact that there would be no immediate rescue, I was astonished to see what looked like an enormous Christmas tree of lights plowing back and forth through the rain and fog. Actually it was a tugboat. I yelled and screamed and waved my arms, but they didn't hear me! In my new panic I almost drowned trying to swim after that boat disappearing in the fog. It was almost an hour before they saw me and hauled me aboard. The elderly skipper of the *Virginia B.* greeted me with tears in his eyes. "I was praying all the time," he said, "but frankly I was looking for a body. I never thought we would find you alive." Then looking me over carefully, he added—unnecessarily from my point of view, "My God, I've never seen such stamina in an old man."

Later I found out that my resourceful daughter had used her orange shelling bag to signal the tugboat as it was hurrying by toward port.

Who Is Ready for Help?

In this traumatic experience of being helped I was aware of many conflicting and complicated feelings. While I was enormously glad to be rescued, I found myself a little chagrined. In one sense I was almost angry at my rescuers. And I couldn't imagine what an ungrateful lout that made me. But before the tug had come along I had resolved to make it back to shore *on my own* as soon as the tide changed and the storm subsided. This would have been a more face-saving solution to my predicament. I felt I had gotten into this situation through my own stupidity. First, I hadn't secured the boat properly, and then when it drifted off in the middle of the storm I foolishly jumped in and swam after it. This kind of seamanship could make me a laughing stock in my little nautical community. But the tug interrupted those plans. And now I couldn't hide my dumb behavior from anyone—and strange as it may seem, my feelings of gratitude were tinged with a little resentment and a good deal of embarrassment.

Helping Is Not a Simple Matter

Through that experience in the Gulf of Mexico I have been more aware than ever of the complications involved in trying to help someone else. For instance, I was amazed at my own resistance to being helped—even though the help may have saved my life. One of Sigmund Freud's most pivotal and monumental discoveries about people was that we all resist help at a certain level. After years of developing his psychoanalytical techniques, he concluded that there is something in all people called "resistance." This seemed the only explanation for the great number of counselees who paid his large fees and yet forgot appointments, came late, lied about details in their case history, or withheld significant information altogether. Even though they appeared to be eager for his help, their behavior indicated that at some level they didn't want to be helped to change at all.

In all of us there seems to be a deep resistance to help, even loving help, or, in fact, to almost any kind of change. Freud found that often this unconscious resistance to being helped is expressed in negative and hostile feelings toward the therapist. Or to put it another way, frequently we develop a dislike for the very people who are trying most desperately to help us. And as Christians going out to love people, I saw that we need to be aware that there are certain ways of giving help that may make it much more easy and pleasant to receive.

Styles of Helping

I have recently been exploring my own feelings toward people who have tried to love me and help me over the years. This has brought to mind feelings I had as far back as kindergarten and first grade when the older children or adults attempted to set me straight as to the official or unofficial rules of life. I recall feeling inferior and resentful on so many of these occasions. It didn't seem to matter that these people meant well—I felt foolish, ignorant, and stupid and wished they would leave me alone. I'm sure I was very difficult to help.

On the other hand, I remember a very positive experience of being helped when I was six or seven years old. I can picture the very house and neighborhood in which it happened. As an only child of elderly parents who as I said earlier were both also Swedish immigrants, I had to acquire all my American street lore from my peers.

And in those days the popular street gadget was a clothespin gun which would shoot rubber bands cut from strips of an old inner tube. As much as I wanted such a gun, I had no way of knowing how to go about building one. I was thrilled when an older friend in the neighborhood asked me to help him make his. I watched the whole process carefully and learned how to make a rubber gun of my very own. I had a feeling of pride and growth as I looked at what I had made. That for me is a dramatic example of being helped by someone who was not consciously trying to help me at all.

To me this incident bears telling because it represents a pattern for helping—one which has been meaningful in my life through the years since. Down through my adolescence, adult years, and now into middle age, the people who have helped me most dramatically are people who were, I feel sure, not conscious of trying to help me. They were with me as friends, not as superior beings. But the people who have been trying more obviously to rescue me from my stupidity, ignorance, stubbornness, meanness, or blindness have probably received more resentment than gratitude.

The incident in the storm made me starkly aware of how much I resist being rescued or helped even now. I am so much like that woman in the commercial who yells at her mother in exasperation, "Please, mother, I'd rather do it myself!" I guess I am the kind of person who gives even God a difficult time as he tries to help me. I suspect that for all of us there are times when, however grateful we are for help, our gratitude may be mixed with resentment and embarrassment.

Respecting the Autonomy of the Person We're Helping

Recently a concerned friend has been trying to help me by bringing about a reconciliation between me and someone who, from my perspective, had used and abused me. It upset my friend to see two people he loved out of communication, so he took a number of steps to bring us together. Actually, I had chosen to terminate the relationship in question because it had become intolerable. I deeply resented these reconciliation attempts and felt I was being denied the autonomy of my choice, which was to live without reconciliation—at least for the time being. So my helping friend felt rejected and so did I, as I exercised my autonomy.

It seems this is exactly the autonomy God gives us. We can choose to live without faith, without love, without friendship, without even God himself—and that's what hell is all about. God does not force us to be saved or helped. He offers us life but he does not manipulate any of us into a "healthy attitude." And although I felt guilty about my attitude, I really resented my friend's attempt to manipulate me into doing the "right thing."

Of course there are times when people are in such desperate need that we help them without thinking of their permission—as when someone has been seriously injured in a wreck or is drowning. But most of the time, it is very important to consider the feelings of autonomy and freedom of the people we are helping.

Dr. Thomas Szasz, teaching psychiatrist at Upstate Medical Center in Syracuse, gave a lecture to a graduating class of doctors which stressed the importance of their helping style in medicine with regard to the patient's feelings. In his concluding remarks, he told them to remember that in the course of their lifetime practice they would meet many people who would prefer illness and even possible death rather than submit to medical treatment which robbed them of their dignity.

You Can't Act for Another

One day Hazel and I had lunch with a couple whom we have come to love a great deal in recent years. Over the years the wife has had recurrent bouts of mental illness, and each time she has had the best and most expensive care, but progress had always been painfully slow. On this particular occasion she seemed her old self again. Being clinically oriented, I asked her what she thought was the turning point in her remarkable recovery. She looked up from her lunch and said very calmly and with great poise, "I began to get well when I said to myself, 'Enough! It's time to move on!'"

Over the years a good many well-meaning and highly paid people had tried to rescue her from her condition. But some way, through some mysterious moving of the spirit, something happened within which finally enabled her to say, "Enough" and to cooperate with her helpers. Not everyone comes to such a clear-cut decision, but it has helped me to realize the enormous power God can release for healing when the one needing help decides to take responsibility for getting well.

Many People Are Not Even Conscious of Their Need for Help

Dostoevsky wrote in *Notes from Underground,* "Every man has reminiscences which he would not tell to everyone but only to his friends. He has other matters in his mind which he would not reveal even to his friends, but only to himself, and that in secret. But there are other things which a man is afraid to tell even to himself, and every man has a number of such things stored away in his mind. The more decent he is the greater number of such things in his mind."

We need to be constantly aware of the fact that there are people all around us who will never demonstrate or admit to their pain because it is too deep and too threatening to face. Their pain comes from the hidden thoughts and feelings Dostoevsky describes. Sometimes we are able to help best by being the nonthreatening kind of person with whom others can explore their crippling, negative and guilt-ridden thoughts. But sometimes if we want to be truly loving, we must approach very slowly and listen because people have had experiences which make them fear personal encounters.

Just down the street from us live a lady and her two Scottie dogs, Whiskers and Thistle. These two dogs have become my special friends in the last four years. The female dog, Thistle, is very outgoing and friendly and seems always eager to have a new relationship. Her brother, Whiskers, is shy and afraid of strangers. It took me three years to win his confidence so that he will now allow me to pet him.

One day I asked my neighbor about this difference between brother and sister. She said, "I really don't know." I pressed her, "Something must have happened to make him so different since they are from the same litter and raised by the same mistress." After thinking a long time she said, "Well, something unusual did happen to him. When he was riding in the car as a very small puppy, someone accidentally closed an electric window on his testicles. His injury required surgery." Many of us are probably like Whiskers. We are shy and aloof because we have been deeply hurt in the past. You cannot pry or force help on us. We are waiting for someone who will take the time and care to inch closer bit by bit and in time perhaps provide a climate where those destructive feelings, thoughts, or experiences from the past can be talked about and more creative actions begun.

The Imperative of Helping

As Christians, all of us are called to be priests, enablers, liberators, servants, and loving helpers, though not necessarily professional ones. In trying to live the adventure of faith and be obedient to Jesus Christ we have no choice but to love people by helping them. He told us that it is more blessed to give than to receive; we are warned that if we try to save our life, we lose it, but if we lose our life, we find it; Jesus urged us to love one another as he has loved us, and his love for us is a sensitive, saving and healing love which leaves people their dignity and freedom. And he commanded us to love in the same way he did and people would know we are his disciples (John 13:35). So as Christians, we have no choice but to be involved in giving, rescuing, saving, helping other people in as sensitive a way as possible.

All around us there are people who are suffering and struggling in tangible and discernible pain. These people are often crying out to be helped even though neither their desire for help nor their gratitude may be expressed directly.

MEMORANDUM

TO: Keith

FROM: Bruce

RE: Chapter Two—How Come It's So Complicated?

Dear Keith,

You and I have often talked about our negative reactions to feeling we are someone else's project. If we are called by God to love and help those around us, how can we do that without having them feel they are our project? I know you have learned a lot about how to do this beginning with simply learning to listen. Would you sketch in some of these suggestions? I hope you'll also tackle the problem of feeling put upon when in a helping situation and how to deal with what may turn out to be unreasonable demands on our time and energy.

I got a letter today addressed to Keith Larson telling me how much the writer enjoyed **Taste of New Wine.** I wrote back to say I wish **I had** written it!

Bruce

Like Bruce, after I had made a serious and specific commitment of my life to God, there was a change in the way I experienced the people and familiar sounds and sights around me. There was a sense of newness. It was like smelling the moist earth after a spring rain. I enjoyed the ordinary things of life more—like tasting food and seeing sunsets. And I was engulfed by a wave of gratitude because I felt as if I were a child who'd found out he was "loved by the teacher."

Since my whole life had centered on a silent and partially unconscious plea to the world to "please love me," this waking up in the mornings with the sense that *God* loved me was almost overwhelming.

Life had always been such a frantic search for immediate direction and achievement that I'd never really had a long-range sense of where I was going. And now in feeling loved by God, I felt that if I would try to live out my commitment to Jesus Christ in the midst of my daily work and relationships, he would lead me to wherever I was supposed to arrive over the long haul. And the details, like what kind of work I did, etc., didn't seem important at all by comparison. But living for God meant loving people, and I found that very difficult and complicated for me.

Almost at once I saw why I have always been a poor lover of other people. I've been afraid they would discover *my* unlovableness. And if I am unlovable how could my love mean anything to them? So I've mostly withheld myself.

But as it began to get through to me that *God,* who invented the Whole Show, loved *me,* something began to open deep inside my inner life. Where I had felt cold, I began to feel a little warm. That center deep within me, which had been closed tight like a new rosebud, began to open like a flower in the warmth of the Holy Spirit's presence in my life. I *was loved!* And he knew all about me!—all my selfish, manipulative ways, my greedy and lustful thoughts, and enormous but hidden pride. He knew it all, and yet he loved me!

37

The night that unbelievable love and acceptance really got through to me, I was up late by myself reading. I walked outside and looked up at the stars in the night. I felt the hot tears of gratitude rise from behind my eyes and overflow, streaming down my face. I took a deep breath and let it out with a long, relaxed sigh. All I could do was shake my head and say "thank you" over and over. I don't know how long I stood there, but it was very late and I was cold when I finally came to myself. I looked up one last time and, cupping my hands, shouted at the top of my lungs to the sky above the sleeping neighborhood, "Thank you, God!" and went back in. The last thought I remember before dropping off to sleep that night was, "God really does love me! He really does!"

Some Conditions Which Make Becoming a Lover of Others More Likely

It seems important to tell you about that feeling of being loved, since I've come to believe that our ability to love other people in healthy ways is almost directly related to whether or not we feel loved by at least one important other. It seems that our gratitude at being saved from the land of the unloved makes us want to open our hands and give away what we've found.

If this is true, then loving other people will not be so much a matter of working hard as it will be of becoming aware of God's love for us and responding to him by committing our lives to Christ and to loving people. And since this kind of loving is impossible to manufacture authentically on our own, one must sometimes just wait until he or she hears and grasps that God loves him or her.

Having tried to "feel loving" toward people out of guilt and failed, I finally noticed that under certain conditions I found myself loving other people very naturally. When these conditions were operative I would find myself (as Bruce did) wanting to reach out to people as I walked around our city and tell them that God loved them—that I loved them. I felt full of an energy for loving which made me want to help people as they struggled with their needs and sins and limitations.

Here are some of the "conditions" which made loving people more natural and spontaneous for me:

(1) *I had to feel secure about my own ultimate destiny*—that I

was going to be with God forever whether I failed or succeeded at my vocation. When that awareness was filling my life, I found myself reaching out with thoughtfulness and sensitivity to people I wouldn't have even noticed before. I would be more generous without worrying so much about what they might do for me in return.

(2) *I had to feel the acceptance of me by some other Christians* in a small group where we were beginning to know each other, warts and all. When I felt understood and loved by those people each week, I found a freedom *away from them* to pay closer attention to the needs of people around me. It was as if the group, made up of those people I met with at 6:30 on Monday mornings, "went with me" like the cloud which followed the Hebrews across the desert—only this was a cloud of everyday men and women. The late Carlyle Marney used to explain that feeling this way: The Freudians, he said, had emphasized the point that we are controlled by basement people from our past (like parents) who go with us everywhere and reach up out of our unconscious to push us off our best trails. He pointed out that we Christians have another powerful kind of influence available to us: people who love God and love us and who go with us in an imaginary balcony on the inside wall of our minds. And they cheer us on to be loving and like Christ when we are out in the world alone—and are tempted to cop out. Our small group became my first live balcony people. And it became very important to me to have a group to be accountable to if the inner gates of unselfish and passionate loving were to stay open when I was away from my Christian friends.

(3) I found that I could keep the loving gates open *by reading even a few lines in the Bible and the lives and works of some of the church's saints* every day. As I read about others who had known God's love and presence, my own experience of feeling loved was verified and renewed. And as I filled my mind with the struggles and faith of those strong and committed people who had gone before me, I was not so likely to drift back into my own greedy and self-serving behaviors. The old picture of a coal dying out when separated from the fire became a real living image. And I also saw that the saints in the Bible and in the church's history could become part of my balcony people through their written words, urging me to keep the faith and love in the world. In my imagination I could take people like Paul and Augustine with me, as I tried to love those I met away from the group.

Some Foundations for Loving Others

There are as many specific ways to express the love that God gives us as there are people who try. And we'll talk about a lot of these later. But there is a process that seems to come with wanting to be a committed Christian, that helps determine the particular shape "loving the world" will take for each of us. The process has to do with wanting to know the truth about ourselves. When we know who we really are behind our facades, we can love people in ways which are more natural for us—and thus more honest and effective.

I have always defended myself against criticism. I was terribly afraid of it for years. I suppose my fear was that I would find out that what I did or was would be proven to be foolish, ignorant, or in some other way unacceptable to *me*. Then I'd be in hopeless despair—if even I didn't approve of me. But when I felt loved by God, just as I was, with no guarantees to change, my reaction over the months and years has been to *want* to find out where my life and work are out of line with God's purposes. And since I believe he has made me with certain gifts and natural inclinations, I *want* to find out those behaviors I have developed which hide my true self and which I use neurotically to win people's love. I want to discover my faults and hangups because I *want to* change my unreal and sinful behaviors to please the One who loves me and is saving me from separation and death.

So I began trying to change and become what I could discover is God's will for me to be. And as I discover more of my authentic self, I am finding more effective and natural ways for me to *love other people specifically.*

Listening

For instance, I talk a lot. And I tried to help people by talking. But I learned that my talking is often a defense against intimacy and being loved. So I began to concentrate on listening to people, particularly people who are in trouble. And with that habit I began to become more natural and apparently more effective with my loving of people in the world—even though I might later help by talking.

Some of the things I am learning about the forms of Christian loving are not nearly as dramatic as I would have expected them to be. Some things I already knew, like the fact that listening with genuine interest is *received by the one being heard* as perhaps one of the deepest experiences of *being loved.* And regardless of what kind of loving help you may be bringing—from food to emergency medical care or spiritual counseling—a listening attitude is the *foundation* for all other loving and helping.

But I learned that if I really want to give away the wonderful gift I'd received of feeling loved by God, that my *listening* was the best way to begin to share it. This is true because people don't feel loved until they are known and understood. And since listening is the fastest way to begin to know and understand someone, it is one of the shortest hallways between two souls for delivering God's love.*

Presence

Since I have always been so proud and afraid to make a fool of myself trying to do things I don't know how to do, I was afraid to talk about God's love for fear I'd fail or look foolish. Just realizing that listening in a certain way is loving was a great help. But as I tried to find other ways to love people, I discovered a simple truth which turned out to be one of the cornerstones for trying to communicate God's love: our very *presence* in a troubled or broken person's life can bring amazing and effective love and help—whether or not we know what to say or even what we are doing as Christian helpers. I have always hesitated to walk into people's lives to help them when I don't feel adequate to give them answers or change things for them. And as a new Christian I felt the same way—although I now felt that I *should* know what to do and say. But I didn't. I thought, "Who am I to visit the sick as a lay person, or to go to the jails? I wouldn't know what to say or do." At least these were my excuses. Besides, I have known some nosy, talkative busybodies who always wanted to help everyone, and instead became burdens and bores. Such people turned me off so much that I didn't want to be identified as one of them; I couldn't see any particular good they were doing by their "visiting the sick," for instance. But then

---

* It sounds here as if I learned to do all these things after I became a Christian. That's not true. But I became aware of what I was doing and how these things were related to God's kind of loving and helping after I tried to commit my life to God.

I remembered something that happened years ago which made me realize the strengthening power we can bring into a situation simply by our *presence*—even if we don't have any words of wisdom or a corrective plan.

It was 1950. My father had just died. Many people came by that night to talk to us and to express their sympathy. Mother was pretty upset, and I was busy trying to serve coffee and help the guests feel at home. My stomach was in a knot. I couldn't cry, though my body ached to. There were other women helping my mother, so I felt I had to put on a front as the man of the house, since I was the only male left. People of all kinds expressed sympathy and offers of help, which were greatly appreciated.

When everyone had left that night except one man, I really saw him for the first time. He was sitting on one end of the couch in the living room, holding a Stetson hat in his lap. He was a tall, wiry man with brown, leathery skin and white hair—looking like the classic picture of a rancher, very different from the other people who had come. I had seen him out of the corner of my eye but hadn't noticed him say a word all evening. When everyone else had left, he stood up, walked over to me, and said very simply and directly, "Son, I knew your daddy and he was a fine man." He looked me in the eyes, shook hands, and turned around and left. I have never forgotten that man, and I can't remember anyone else who came to call that night. The fact that he came and sat with us in our grief all evening without having to say a thing, then finally made a comment about my dad and left was enough. That man had come for my father and for us. I can't even remember his name, but his presence had an enormous effect on me.

From then on when anyone I knew well lost a loved one through death, I tried to go to the funeral—sometimes traveling great distances simply to be with people I love when they were going through a time of grief. I realize now that most of the time it doesn't matter much what I say, if I can only be present. I think this is a basic truth about visiting people who are sick and perhaps even those in prison: it is not so important that you come with an articulate and convincing message as that you come and care. So few people do that, you might have opportunities to help and love people that would be far beyond anything you could imagine, judged by the criteria we usually apply to this situation.

Resistance to Loving Others

Learning about these two positive foundation aspects of almost any loving encounter—listening and "presence"—can make a big difference in our ability to help other people. But what about the strange resistances we may discover in *ourselves* to *helping?*

As I began listening and being present to people outside my own family I began to feel like a healthier person and more authentic as a Christian. I liked myself better, and also was experiencing the world as a much richer and warmer place. But I recognized almost at once that there was a great resistance in me to reaching out in this way. For one thing, I was afraid I might have to "take them to raise," that is, if I helped people once, they might think I was going to be their lifelong friend and counselor and then show up on my doorstep every morning. And if they did, I knew I wouldn't be able to get rid of them or get my work done. I know that sounds incredibly selfish and un-Christian, but it is true.

Overcoming Resistances by Setting Realistic Limits

However, I soon found that when I am honest and direct about my helping, those things I feared about being overwhelmed by people almost never happen. For instance, if someone calls from another town and wants to come spend a day talking about his problems and I must work, I say "No, I can't spend a day. But I could talk to you between four and five thirty"—or whatever time I can realistically see him or her. Sometimes I have to tell such persons that because of previous commitments I'm sorry, we'll have to arrange a later time, or try to suggest a way they can get help in their own town.

Or if a transient needs help to get from one city to another, I might buy him or her a bus ticket, saying, "This is all the financial help I am going to give you, but I can do this." Then if the person writes for more money (and it does not feel right to send it), I say I cannot, and I don't feel guilty that I can't be everything for everybody.

What I'm suggesting is that it seems helpful to everyone involved when I set realistic limits on the loving help I can give. Then people are not as likely to feel rejected when I reach those realistic limits regarding my time. Of course in certain emergencies you may break all your limits. But it will be *your decision under God* and not a neurotic, guilt-triggered succumbing to pressure.

There are times when a very busy helper must make the decision *not* to help at all, I think, when he is already committed to an inordinate number of people and problems. For several years there were periods I was so exhausted I felt I might actually do harm by getting involved with another person. But I think these times are not nearly as many as I rationalize them to be. Often I *keep* myself too busy for the kind of interruption Jesus always seems to have had time for. I think the commandment to love must continue to ring down the halls of our minds and down the corridors of our churches until we hear it and adjust our lives so that we can answer it as the rule and not the exception in our life. But I do believe we must learn when and how to say "no" in order to keep from destroying our families and other primary relationships by being totally available to strangers. Jesus certainly felt free to take off from the press of people in the midst of his ministry (e.g., Matt. 14:23).

In summary, when I feel loved by God, and keep experiencing that love on a regular basis through a local group of balcony friends, I can sometimes find the courage and support to love other people. And when I'm joined by heroes and heroines of the faith through my devotional reading, I can listen to people better and be present to them; I can love more passionately and realistically in situations away from my Christian friends. And on some days, when these conditions exist, loving doesn't seem quite as complicated.

Chapter Three

What Motivates a Good Samaritan?

MEMORANDUM

TO: Bruce

FROM: Keith

RE: Chapter Three—What Motivates a Good Samaritan?

Dear Bruce,

In thinking about this chapter I've had to really ask myself some searching questions about my own motivations for loving people. And in looking back over my life a lot of the answers I came up with don't make me very proud of myself.

It's always seemed to me that you are a natural-born helping person. I wish you'd tell a little about how you feel concerning your own attempts at being a good Samaritan. What have you learned about lovingly helping people for Christ's sake? Your early conditioning and helping style? Your motives? Your feelings when helping? Helping the "undeserving"? And maybe something about the relationship of a commitment to Jesus Christ to the quality of your loving in the world?

In this brief space, there's no way we can even touch the wide range of different motives, styles of helping and subtle ways we miss being like the model Jesus gave us for loving. But just trying to raise some of these questions has already stirred me to check my own motives and ways of loving. This book is beginning to make me take a new look at my life—and it's making me a little nervous.

I hope you can deal with some of the above.

Keith

I am an incorrigible helper; I like to love people by helping them—it makes me feel good. On a purely selfish basis I have usually found helping a rewarding experience. That's the way I am conditioned to be.

Recently, as my wife Hazel and I were discussing this predisposition—which is sometimes almost an obsession—we recalled some of my brilliant excesses of helping in the past. She reminded me of an incident that happened in our first church. We had been married a little over two years, had two babies in diapers and were living in a one bedroom apartment. One day a stranger turned up at the church saying that he was a minister, defrocked because of demon possession, and he needed help. My response was something like, "Pilgrim, your search has ended. You've come to the right place."

I assured him that I believed in demons and in Jesus' power of deliverance. I still do, though the definition of demons might need clarifying. At that point, he gestured over his shoulder toward his wife and four preschool children sitting in a road-weary old car. I realized he was asking where they might stay while I was helping him with his demon problem. I promptly invited them all into the little apartment where the four Larsons were living.

The first thing they did was haul baskets of dirty clothes in from the car. I don't think our washer and dryer stopped running during their entire stay. After three days, my wife suggested that we move to a friend's house and give our guests the apartment. And after six days of unsuccessful attempts to exorcise the demon with no hint that they would ever be moving on, I finally, somewhat firmly, helped them on their way with a tank of gas and a picnic lunch. As they disappeared around the corner at the end of our street, I should have begun to suspect my "good Samaritanism" could use a little less zeal and a lot more judgment.

In that same congregation was a young divorcee with three children. Alimony had stopped coming and she needed to work. We were in a small prayer group with her, and we all prayed that God would send a babysitter she could afford so she could work. When an elderly lady finally turned up, we were convinced she was the answer to our prayers, though she seemed frail and somewhat addled. Her first day on the job, I stopped in to assure her of my concern. If I could do anything to help, she was to let me know. Two days later she called. The toilet was stopped up and would I please rush over and bring a plunger? This sort of thing occurred regularly, but I never had the heart to tell her that this kind of help was not exactly what I'd had in mind. I'd anticipated helping with more spiritual problems. Again I had to check my motives—and what I was really saying with my offers to help.

Over the years my "good Samaritanism" has frequently prompted me to find employment for out-of-work friends or even strangers. This vocational matchmaking can be fraught with unpleasant consequences. If the matchmaking is less than happy (and what match is always entirely happy?), the matchmaker catches a lot of resentment from both parties—perhaps justly so. At any rate, I think I'm finally cured from the sort of indiscriminate matchmaking which stems from my need to be the one who rearranges people's lives.

Looking back over my life, I realize I've gotten into a lot of peculiar situations because of my need to make a magnanimous gesture without thinking it through. What will it cost me? How does it affect my other commitments? Will the end result be resentment or real growth for the person I am helping—and for me? And, most important, is this God's will for me?

Now I am learning to resist my first impulses. I no longer automatically rush in to help. I believe God wants us all to be helpers, but I must find out what he is saying in a given situation and how I may give help that will be of real benefit to the other person and leave me feeling grateful for the experience—regardless of how difficult it may have been.

Early Conditioning and Your Helping Style

But what makes a good Samaritan? Why are some people conditioned to help while other people find it so very difficult? Perhaps it is because we are programmed or conditioned as children to define help in different ways. We have vastly different views on what help is and who needs it. One view is probably best summed up by the phrase "a frontier mentality," an attitude typical of western settlers of more than a hundred years ago. Many men and women of pioneer spirit left their own little piece of civilization and moved into a wilderness to build a log cabin or sod hut with their bare hands and carve out a living for themselves and their children. Some did not survive because of weather, animals, illness, or hostile Indians. But those who did passed on to their children an unconscious view that people at their best are self-reliant creatures. These early do-it-yourselfers didn't accept help except in dire emergencies and they were not prepared to offer help except as a last resort. For them, to offer help—except in certain situations like rebuilding a house after a fire—was to patronize and demean the other person.

I was raised by people with this mind-set. As I said earlier, both of my parents were born in Sweden. For a time we lived in a Swedish ghetto in Chicago. My parents' closest friends were Swedish immigrants, and they belonged to a club made up of Swedish immigrants. In 1933 when the newly elected Franklin D. Roosevelt began to institute programs whereby the government took responsibility for feeding people and providing jobs, my parents and their friends were outraged. They had come from a foreign land with no money in their pockets and no contacts and no knowledge of English and had made it on their own. The very idea of government help was demeaning. But I would like to think this attitude evolved less from stinginess or selfishness than from a deep awareness of every person's need for human dignity.

On the other hand, some of you may have grown up in homes where your parents were the unofficial pastors, counselors, and welfare officers for the entire neighborhood. Your mother was the person making chicken soup and casseroles for every wedding, funeral, illness, or bar mitzvah. Your father was the neighborhood moneylender or handyman or job-finding bureau. Strays slept all over the house on sofas or on makeshift beds. Perhaps your parents considered themselves responsible for anyone in need and readily shared time, money, food, and advice. Obviously, a child growing up in this environment is likely to be programmed to view Christian helping in much the same way—unless the child rejects his parents, in which case he or she might adopt an opposite attitude toward loving people.

Mixed Signals

But sometimes our conditioning is blurred. In my case, even though my parents were violently against "the dole" (government help to individuals) I remember a steady stream of broken men being fed on our back porches all through the depression. No one who asked for food was ever turned away. Wherever we lived, our house bore the secret mark made by hobos that said a kind lady lived inside. So it is no wonder I am programmed to be a helper.

I'm beginning to realize that it's no wonder couples have different ideas about what appropriate helping is—even in the same marriage.

Some Examples of Different Helping Styles

Let's take a look at a helping situation and examine some of the responses we may be programmed to make. For example, let's say you are the only witness to a hit-and-run accident on a lonely street at midnight. You decide to leap into your car and pursue the hit-and-run driver. You are determined to collar the offender and bring him or her to justice. In the meantime, of course, the victim lies unaided and may even be dying. On the other hand, in the same situation, perhaps you are programmed immediately to care for the victim, apply first-aid and call for an ambulance. In the first case, you are apprehending a criminal and you may be saving future victims. In the second instance, you may be saving a life and you are acting in the best interests of the wounded person. Both kinds of help are needed. And most of us are conditioned to give one kind or the other—unless, of course, we are conditioned to pass by on the other side of the street and not get involved at all.

One day a few months ago I received letters from two Christian friends who are practicing their vocation as helpers very differently. One is a married woman with a handicapped son. This young mother has an enormous capacity for helping people. Almost every letter bears fresh news of someone she has taken into her life—and usually into her home—because they need help.

Recently she wrote, "Several months ago a prayer partner called and asked for prayers for a Christian home situation for a young American Indian teenager named Anna who had spent a year in a reformatory home for problem children. Anna had progressed to the point where the authorities were convinced that if she did not have the opportunity to function in a regular home situation, she might soon become 'institutionalized,' but she had no home to go to. Her mother is an alcoholic. Anna has four brothers and sisters, none of whom have the same father. She and her siblings have been shifted from one foster home to another. After Anna had run away several times, and been placed in other foster homes, the tribe finally gave up and sent her to a reform school.

"As I was praying for this young woman, it seemed like I became aware that our home would be the ideal place for her. I am tied down with our son, so whenever she came home from school, a mother figure would be on deck to greet her, love her, hear her problems, and really care. When my husband called home, I asked him if we could do this, and after some discussion, he agreed."

As far as I know, that young Indian girl is still in my friend's home. The girl is making progress, but she still has deep-seated problems. However, she now has a home and a future because of the way one woman was conditioned to help. But for other equally committed Christians, it might seem very inappropriate to disrupt a home and family life by having live-in people with serious emotional problems.

My other correspondent is a certified public accountant in a large town in Iowa. He and I have talked on the phone about his dreams for the future, and this letter was a follow-up to those conversations. "Although it is quite presumptuous of me, I feel that there is definitely a method by which we can effectively eliminate poverty in the United States. The method that I advocate would be completely accomplished by the private sector and would not require any government involvement. . . . In my judgment, the logical group to make the thing go would be a church or congregation because it is the sort of thing that churches ought to become involved in." He then outlined a very detailed, yet simple plan whereby a single church congregation could begin to work toward the elimination of poverty in its immediate area and ultimately in the world.

All types of helpers are desperately needed at every level. The important thing is that each of us should be involved in the kind of help and change which is best suited to us as persons—which may well be the kind for which we were conditioned.

Four Motives for Helping

We have already discussed the fact that our offers to help are sometimes rejected. Occasionally it's because they are made in such a way that the other person feels patronized. Or, our reasons for helping can stem from wrong motives and this is sensed by the person we are trying to help.

Let me suggest at least four very different motives that one can have for getting involved with another person in a helping situation. *First,* there are people who help only reluctantly or *under coercion.* These people live to and for themselves, almost as hermits. They ignore the needs of others unless those needs correspond with their own. They are motivated to help only by the threat of court action or some other form of not-so-friendly persuasion. I should say, however, that this negative form of helping is not all bad. For example, back in the sixties, militant black leaders told me they preferred to negotiate with white bigots about racial issues because at least they knew where they stood with them and, consequently, expected nothing extra from them when they were grudgingly changing their institutions to conform to the law. I interpret this to mean that occasionally people who are not your friends may be forced by circumstances to give genuine help even though they are unwilling to do so.

Second, we may be moved to help out of a *sense of duty.* We help because of parental influences, philosophical injunctions, or from a genuine sense of Christian ethics. Deep inside we feel that it is our duty to help people.

The problem with the duty motive, as I see it, is that we tend to see people as projects, and we certainly don't see them as people who may one day be on their feet and perhaps even be strong enough to give us help. In past years the colonialists in Africa generally operated from this motive. They helped the indigenous people only because they felt it was their duty, their burden as civilized people to do so. The classic term "the white man's burden" sums up the helping stance of the colonialists of those times.

This kind of "duty-helping" often involves a legalism of which I find myself guilty sometimes. I am tempted to use my good deeds to justify myself. Enough such good deeds will cancel out any dishonesties or excesses. Perhaps this earning our own righteousness is the thing that makes it distasteful to be on the receiving end of the dutiful giver. We suspect that such efforts are being used to justify the giver or his or her self-seeking or indulgent way of life. And we resent this modern day method of buying indulgences.

A *third* motive for helping others is *personal pleasure*—it makes you feel good. There are people, in fact a lot of them, who just *enjoy* helping because it can be a way of controlling people and of winning approval. As Keith and I have both said, we often find ourselves helping with this kind of motive. We assume that if we shower others with our attention, gifts, favors, or influence, they are certain to become our grateful friends forever.

But this doesn't always work. Most people resent being in someone else's debt. For this reason anyone who is in a helping role must be careful about giving too much help too fast lest the relationship become unbearable for the other party. Whether you are in the loving, helping role accidentally, as a parent or friend, or whether you are a professional such as a therapist or clergyman, too much dependence puts a strain on the relationship.

We have to be sure that our pleasure in helping doesn't come at the expense of the one being helped. In talking with Paul Tournier recently, I asked him to share his secret for helping others in the counseling situation. He was embarrassed and said, "Oh, Bruce, I don't know how to help people. I simply listen and love and try to provide a safe place where people can come and report on their progress without any judgment." Without doubt, Paul Tournier enjoys helping people, but he has discovered how to be a nonthreatening friend to whom others can come and with whom they can find help in discovering God's next step for their lives—without feeling that Tournier is working off his need to help on them. In this, Dr. Tournier is a refreshing departure from the kind of helpers, clergy or lay, who appear to know all the answers and who have their little kit of fix-it tools ready any hour of the day or night. He not only does not claim to know how to help you, he admits that on certain days he needs help himself.

Although I sometimes have helped out of all the first three motives the *fourth* motive for helping is the one to which I aspire: *to help out of love or compassion.* And I would define love as aggressively wanting someone else's well-being. It is possible that the friend truly concerned about helping me may or may not be able to put his concern into words, and he or she may or may not enjoy helping me in the way I am demanding or needing at the time. But when I am really helped I feel that the one helping is someone who cares about me and who would go to any lengths to supply the kind of help I need.

Helping When It Doesn't Feel Good

When we act out of genuine love or compassion, we are free to help even when it doesn't feel good. There was a time when I felt guilty about this. Once I had a parishioner who continually called me at one or two in the morning when he was drunk. At such times he always wanted to come over and see me and talk about his life and his marriage and God. I would make a pot of coffee and brace myself for sitting up all night. Actually, I felt pretty resentful about missing my sleep in order to listen to still another chapter in his life story told through a slurred and drunken fog.

I finally stopped feeling guilty about my feelings of resentment when it dawned on me that helping doesn't have to feel good. Frankly, I am suspicious of people who would be thrilled to have you call any hour of the day or night, drunk or sober. Now I would probably see the person long enough that night to make an appointment the next day, since I find very little constructive help takes place when the one seeking help is drunk.

An incident from the Book of Acts has helped me a good deal in this area of helping when it doesn't feel good. We read that when Paul and Barnabas were out preaching the gospel a disturbed slave girl began to follow them around shouting incessantly that she knows who they are—"servants of the most high God." Eventually, Paul healed her, much to the anger of her owners, who were deprived of her earnings as a fortune-teller. Now, I had always assumed that Paul healed her out of compassion and sympathy. But Luke the physician records the healing with these words, "Paul was so annoyed by her that he healed her in Jesus' name" (Acts 16:18). Paul was able to call down the Holy Spirit of God to help someone in need whatever his feelings or motives at the moment. I believe that love is acting in someone's best interests whether or not we enjoy it and whether or not we feel like it.

Helping the Undeserving

At times we may get hung up on whether or not someone deserves help. Our daughter is presently living near us in the agricultural center of our state where many migrants live and work. Last Christmas she was asked to take charge of serving Christmas dinner to a number of these people. Christine recruited her brother and some friends to help, and they fed three hundred and sixty needy people. The following day she was discussing the event with an older neighbor who was suspicious of the whole affair. "Don't you know that many of those people are freeloaders?" "But that's just the point," Chris explained. "Dinner was free for anyone who came. They were *all* freeloaders."

When I am guilty of helping on the basis of whether or not people are deserving, I suspect I have missed the whole point. We are all freeloaders. Everyone is deserving and no one is deserving. We all need to be helped and we all need to give help. We help because it is needed. We love because God first loved us. There is no point system or test for worthiness. The good Samaritan never asked for credentials from the robbery victim beside the road.

Most of us who have experienced the reality of God's love come to have a passion to share that love in concrete ways with the rest of humanity. In the twenty-fifth chapter of Matthew Jesus says, "For I was hungry and you gave me food, I was thirsty and you gave me drink, I was a stranger and you welcomed me, I was naked and you clothed me, I was sick and you visited me, I was in prison and you came to me" (vv. 35–36). Regardless of how we may be conditioned to help, Jesus has given us a mandate to be good Samaritans in a world of needs.

MEMORANDUM

TO: Keith

FROM: Bruce

RE: Chapter Three—What Motivates a Good Samaritan?

Dear Keith,

You said on the phone that you would be writing your section on Chapter Three this week.

Don't you sometimes wish we had a psychological profile on the Good Samaritan? I wonder what made him react to need so instinctively, apparently without any concern about his own immediate plans or about the expense of lodging the injured man at the inn.

How do we get motivated as the Good Samaritan was, and particularly to do something "with our name on it?" Can you give a personal example?

I'm going to celebrate finishing my part of Chapter Three by going fishing. My neighbor got a snook yesterday.

Wish you were here.

Bruce

The past three years I've been reexamining almost everything in my life. I've been brooding about my motives for loving other people, for helping them. And I don't like some of the things I've seen. Sometimes I've felt incurably selfish and doubted my own sincerity and that of some of the people around me. I've wrestled with questions I never had to ask myself before: What kind of person am I anyway? And how did I get to be the kind of person I am? How was I conditioned to have the motives I've had for loving? If I find my motives aren't what I think they should be as a Christian, can I ever change? And if my motives have been good but have gotten selfish, how can I get reconditioned to love unselfishly, like the Good Samaritan—the way God would want me to?

When I sat down to write about my own approach to loving people, I thought of my father and mother. The picture which flashed onto the screen of my mind was of my father's funeral. Not long before, my older brother had been killed and as I mentioned I was the last surviving male in our family. It was a sad day. When the people were gone I found myself automatically going through some family business papers trying to get them sorted out for my mother.

I can still see myself in jeans and a tee shirt, sitting on the floor in my parents' bedroom alone. I was reading a box of letters which had come at the time of my father's death. Reading those letters about Earle Miller, the man I'd known as "Dad," seemed strange. Time dissolved and I shrank into an eight-year-old boy again as I sat there in the midst of those boxes. I was surprised at the feelings expressed by people I'd never met. Dad was a person who didn't talk a lot and never made much of a show of anything good that he did. As I went through the letters I began feeling strange emotions. Finally I put my face in my hands and sobbed. Notes had come from people he hadn't seen for 25 years. There were envelopes with checks from men who had borrowed or been given money years before. In one letter there was fifty dollars in cash. The writer of the letter said that Dad had loaned him the money during the depression when the man had been destitute. He'd never told how much the help had meant, but he was always grateful because he knew

57

my father didn't have much when he had given the money. There were letters from different sorts of people who had been touched in their lives by Dad, none of whom I'd known anything about. In a way I was sorry that he hadn't shared some of these things with me. But as it was, I felt that I was seeing a whole new side of my father and the way he had chosen to love people. And as I sat there I hoped I'd become more like him and not make such a show of it when I did something loving or helpful.

Then I thought about my mother and how much she was like my dad in wanting to help, but how different she was in the way she went about it.

Loving People to Win Their Applause—and Their Love

Mother loved to help people, too, and did all the time. But unlike my father she thoroughly enjoyed the feedback—the credit for the good things she did.

For years I was critical of Mother for feeling so good about the response she got from people she helped. Then one day I realized that I'm much more like her than I am my father in this regard. I'm just more subtle about it. I, too, love to get feedback when I help someone. And although my motives have changed a lot the past few years, I still love to hear how much I am appreciated for what I've done. When I first discovered this I was shocked and thought I must be a poor Christian. But a wise friend pointed out that this is natural and very human and further that even *God* seems to want feedback in the form of a response from us when he offers us love and salvation. Somehow, in coming up with a purist idea of loving, I'd forgotten that the helper and the one being loved are in a *relationship* with each other. Of course it's all right for loving feelings of gratitude to be expressed and received in such a relationship.

And I began to see that there is nothing wrong with enjoying the response from the persons I'm loving and helping, as long as that's not the *purpose* of my efforts. I realized that what I had been condemning, perhaps rightly, was lovingly helping people solely to be thought of as a good person. Doing this has been part of my attempt to buy love. But I also saw that during the time I had reacted and criticized my dear mother for "playing to the crowd," *I* had often not been helping people at all as I insisted on my "pure motives." I decided it's better to love people with impure motives than to keep yourself spotless regarding your motives, and not help anyone.

Jesus commented that if we want to love in a way which is most pleasing to God, it would be better for "the left hand not to know what the right hand is doing." I think he knew how easy it is to manipulate people's responses by helping them and being sure they know you did. Then they owe you, and once you get people obligated, it is much easier to control them. And they are doubly frustrated since they feel that they are terrible if they don't love you back and want to help you—because you have been "so good to them." Many of us parents are guilty of this kind of subtle controlling. I have been horrified to realize that I have done this with my daughters.

As I thought about these things I wondered what kind of a mix I am of my mother and father and the way they chose to love people. And I thought back into my childhood and began to realize how my conditioning to love started.

One of my earliest memories as a little boy was having my mother read to me and talk to me about life. She was a good woman, very wise and understanding about the ways of people. She held me on her lap and told me that if I would pay attention to others and listen to them, if I would be interested in their lives, I'd be happier and they would like me. Inside, behind the confident smile on my face, I wanted very much to be loved. So I really took her advice and tried to be interested in other people.

But as I began growing up, things changed. I did well in sports and was accepted as "one of the boys." I sort of forgot about my mother's advice to be interested in other people during the later years of grade school and into the first two years of junior high.

Then, as we approached the ninth grade, there was an election for "the most outstanding boy in school." At that time I was only interested in what I was doing: sports, drama, studying, and girls. But I was almost sure that I'd win the election since it was narrowed down to two of us. The other boy had been a friend for a long time. He was well liked, but he wasn't an athlete, and in our school I simply couldn't imagine his winning—that is, until he did. That night I went home, secretly crushed by the defeat. In my self-centeredness I wondered why a majority of students didn't support me. But as I thought about it and watched my friend, I realized something very important. Although I had been active in a lot of things, he had quietly gone around and gotten to know everybody's name and had helped them in simple small ways.

So when I got to high school that is exactly what I did. My

motives weren't evil. I just practiced what my mother had taught me and I remembered the lesson of the lost election. I got to know almost everybody in the high school of several thousand students and helped a lot of people with their lives and decisions. When I was a senior I held the two highest offices in the school simultaneously and I had made a lot of friends along the way. Even then I remember feeling uneasy about my motives in operating with people. But I had learned well the lesson of loving people in order to win their love, approval—and support.

And this was my primary motive for loving when I became a Christian. Except that I now was trying to win the love and approval of God and of other Christians.

The only trouble was that I felt uneasy when I read about the biblical heroes. They loved people and did God's will because they *loved him*. I had the uneasy feeling that I was loving people for my own sake and through my own strength and willfulness—even though I talked about doing God's will and wanted to. But there was little of the naturalness and the disregard for who got the credit which I saw in people like the Good Samaritan, for instance.*

Loving People "in Faith"

But how does a person who has been conditioned to love people as a bartering to win their love learn to help "in faith" because he or she loves God? I knew how to pull out all the stops and work for Christ. In fact, I'd almost worn myself and my family out with my compulsive working and enormous energy. Until I tried to commit my life to God, I was sort of like a snaking fire hose loose on the sidewalk, knocking people down with the undisciplined stream of energy swishing one way and then another.

In Christ, the energy was becoming focused, but it still seemed to be powered and directed by my own needs. Since I wanted to please my new Christian brothers and sisters—when I finally met some of them—I tried to do what they did, only more and better. And before long I was tired. I also realized that every Christian is not thrilled if you do more and better than he or she. Besides, I realized something was wrong in my life and with my frantic helping. I needed a new motivation to go on.

---

* I realize that the New Testament account does not say that the Good Samaritan was motivated by the love of God. But his behavior and natural, unselfconscious *way* of helping constitute the model Jesus gave us for loving our neighbors.

Different people will have very different stories of how they were led to change their basic approach to loving people. Personally I cannot alter my entrenched behaviors easily. As a matter of fact, I only seem to be able to change direction at all as a result of cataclysmic confrontations in my life. Two such confrontations since I've been a Christian have done a lot to change my motivations for loving and helping.

Facing Death

After I'd been converted a few years, I got very tired of even *being* with people, much less trying to help them. Since I had not been sick or had any kind of major disappointment or failure as a Christian, I couldn't understand why I just seemed to have lost interest in being a loving person.

I got depressed and withdrew from the projects and some of the people I was with. In the solitary introspection which followed I saw that I had become ineffectual, a "tinkling cymbal." A couple of friends died, and I felt very inadequate to help their families as I sat with them. I knew that I was deeply uneasy about something, but didn't know what it was. At last I realized: it was death. I woke up one night in a cold sweat and realized that someday *I* was going to die. I spent three or four days on the edge of panic. I imagined myself in a coffin: not breathing, not thinking, not being. Then I thought of my family. And I realized that almost everyone in my parental family had already died. Finally, after being terrorized by the idea of my own death for a couple of days, I told God I was just going to have to bet everything on him. I told him that what was good enough for my family was good enough for me—even death. And I consciously committed my whole future to God, including my death.

I woke up one morning shortly after that and realized that something in my bedroom was different, more peaceful. Without moving I let my eyes move around the room, but everything was the same, the pictures, the shutters, the wallpaper. Then it hit me. *I* was different. I was relaxed. And I was not terrorized by the idea of my own death any more. I was *very* grateful to God.

During the next few days I began to move back into life and the relationships from which I'd backed off. And I realized that my feelings about loving people had changed. Since I'd now bet my life on God and his ability to handle its ultimate outcome—

even my own death—I didn't feel so much pressure to please other Christians.

I saw what I have told you here; that as a child I had been conditioned to help in ways that would make people love me. But now suddenly as an adult I had faced the fact of my own death and the futility of *any* efforts to earn ultimate love and security. I saw that the only thing that was important was that *God* loved me— since no one else could ultimately save me or even judge me. And this realization that the approval of people can never provide the security I was seeking, this experience was to be the turning point for me toward beginning to love people because God loves me.

I saw that if I am already loved by the most creative and loving Person in the universe, then I do not have to earn love from anyone. If he has showed me that my insignificant life is valuable enough to die for, then for me to barter my helping of people for his approval is preposterous. Maybe I could love God and people simply because I was *grateful* and *happy* to be loved by him. What a *relief* that would be!

I see now how Jesus and many of the Christian martyrs could dare to be misunderstood and die ignominious deaths trying to help people. They were not setting out to win any gold buttons in Sunday school from their fellow Christians or the people they were loving. They were simply loving others because that was what they *wanted* to do for God, realizing that he knew and understood their intentions. And they believed that he would somehow reward them in his kingdom as Jesus said he would (Matt. 25:34).

And when I can do it, this putting my security in God and trying to trust him with the results of my total life gives me a much greater awareness of the people I contact, as real persons. When I am talking to someone who is in trouble during such times, I can see symptoms, difficulties, and creative possibilities of loving them that I cannot see when my mind is blinded by my own frantic efforts to get success or love for myself.

But what if we have been motivated to love as a grateful response to God at one time, but have *lost* that motivation? How can we get it back?

Motivation Reborn—at the End of a Rope

Several years ago I moved to a small island in the Gulf of Mexico in order to write. We attended services at a little chapel, but there was no "church program" as such. I was not in a small group and so felt isolated from other Christians on the adventure of trying to commit their lives to Christ.

Although I didn't see it coming, a kind of hardening of the spiritual arteries started to take place. I was concentrating on my work, but because I wasn't meeting with any "balcony" people in a small group, my writing was not growing out of the live, fresh relationship with the brokenness and pain of the men and women around me. My writing was out of experiences of the past or illustrations picked up on speaking trips. I was working hard, but somehow I wasn't making a sacrifice to love the people in our community who needed God so desperately. My excuse was that I was involved with so many dozens of people through my books and correspondence that I didn't have the emotional space to handle a lot of close relationships any more. And although there was some truth in this, I had gotten my priorities all fouled up and felt somehow undernourished spiritually.

Father William McNamara helped me when he pointed out that all spiritual emotions and high resolves die unless they are nourished. When we luxuriate in the status quo our lives get ruined. As he put it, "Most lives are not ruined through wickedness, but through the gradual gathering of grease and scum when not stirred by sacrifice."[1]

I realize now that I had backed off from the work I had somehow felt assigned by God to do: to relate intimately to people for Christ's sake. This resulted in a kind of sin and separation that I never could have seen had I not been confronted deeply through the circumstances of my life. Relationships very close to me got cracked and then shattered, and to my horror I could not put things back together again as I had always been able to do. Finally in 1976 my wife and I were divorced. And I wanted to run and hide from everyone.

In the storm that followed in my own mind and heart, I questioned every motivation I'd ever had. I wondered if I had ever done anything for God. Being divorced, I was afraid of the rejection of other Christians who might not be able to understand or accept sin and error in a "Christian writer." I had to decide if I were going to trust Christ and his forgiveness—which had been the deepest motivation I'd had to help others. I smiled grimly when I realized how right C. S. Lewis was in saying, "You never know how much you really believe anything until its truth or falsehood becomes a matter of life and death to you. It is easy to say you believe a rope to be strong and sound as long as you are merely using it to cord a box. But suppose you had to hang by that rope over a precipice. Wouldn't you first discover how much you really trusted it?"[2]

In life it seems that we often topple over the precipice and have to grab the rope without ever having a chance to give it the ultimate test ahead of time. As I began to work through the brokenness and come to grips with myself, I saw very clearly in my motivations and in my life faults that had only been dim shadows before. I saw some of the things I've written here about my unconscious self-centeredness as a Christian in helping other people in order to be known and loved. And I was ashamed.

I saw that I had been given enough abilities to handle almost all the problems in my life up to that time. And yet I could not pretend that I had not been divorced. I could not pretend that I was not a failure as a husband. I could no longer tell myself that all was well when I saw that I had denied to myself my own feelings and needs for years. And I could not make right what was not right in my own home. This was an enormous shock and ego insult to me, not to be able to rationalize or excuse my sin and failure.

But out of this experience has come a new motivation. I am so grateful for a second chance at life that I cannot express my gratitude to God enough. Somehow again the freshness of Christ's love has become very close to me on the brighter edge of sadness and the failure of my integrity as a Christian. I am able to hear individuals and am strongly motivated to work with small groups of people, finding out how to live and love on the adventure with Christ.

I am beginning to see that the renewed motivation God can give us to help others seems to come as a result of our facing our own sin, confessing and making what restitution we can, and thanking him for forgiving us and granting us a new start. Then, when we set out in gratitude to find and do his will, our loving can be empowered by the energy God has given us to live again on the other side of failure. And I believe this process of renewal and reborn motivation to love takes place again and again in a growing Christian's life. So, whether we are bishops, ministers, or laypersons, the recognition of failure and sin can, through Christ, lead us to embrace and thank God for the new life and motivation he has given us to love his world.

Chapter Four

Creative Change and What Produces It

MEMORANDUM

TO: Keith

FROM: Bruce

RE: Chapter Four—Creative Change and What Produces It

Dear Keith,

We have son Mark here just now on a holiday from school and that means the house is filled with full-volume stereo sound.

I'm hoping you'll zero in on change from the perspective of the helper. What are some of the things we can do and be that will encourage other people to take steps toward change and growth? What kind of credentials does such a helper need?

Also, we are sometimes forced into change by circumstances, often through failure. For example, if our marriage fails or we lose our job, we are faced with change. Can you help our readers deal creatively with that kind of change?

Writing this book is making me do a lot of self-examination too.

Bruce

W hen I realized that Christian help is aimed at producing an atmosphere in which noncoercive change can take place, which will lead people to find God's will for their lives, I discovered certain attitudes and approaches that make it most likely that this sort of creative change can take place when I am trying to help people.

An Attitude of Walking with People

My basic feeling is that I am going to "walk with" a person needing help through the midst of his problems. Let's say that I'm dealing with an individual man, for instance. As he points out dangers and fears and describes impossible situations, my primary help at first is to *hear* him so I'll know what *he sees* that scares or blocks his progress in life. My only attempt at "guidance" is a gentle suggestion at certain points in his story to "please stop and describe that more fully" or to ask questions to make sure I am hearing what he's saying: "I'm hearing you say that you are afraid every time your teenaged girl is away from the house. Is that right?" Once we both see his problems from his perspective, then we can either work together to find a solution he can implement, or I can possibly help him to see that another problem may be causing the difficulty. And we may be able to deal with that.

An Attitude of Listening with Imagination

To do this gentle listening, I find a particular attitude is most helpful. In my mind I imagine I'm dealing with my own brother or sister whom I love very much, who is in real trouble, and for whom I want the very best. When I can listen and imagine myself facing the difficulties or agony of the people I'm working with this way, a strange thing may happen, partially described above. And the understanding I begin to feel through listening communicates itself *to them* as a spiritual relaxer. Inner prison walls crumble inside them, and sometimes a hope, a freedom and an energy are released in their lives that enable them to begin to deal with their difficulties

67

and determine God's will for them, even though their problems seem to be massive and impossible at first. It's hard for people who haven't tried to listen this way to appreciate the awesome power of really being listened to and heard by someone who really cares about you.

Don't Judge but Don't Cop Out

One of the main reasons I've always hated to ask for help is that I've been afraid the person helping me will uncover something in me that will be so embarrassing it will make me look terrible and inadequate. I've been afraid the helper would judge me for failures or sins which were involved in my needing help. And I think many other people who need help feel that we Christians may be *most* likely to frown on their mistakes or sins—particularly if they involve any moral failures.

Jesus evidently didn't make people feel judged in this way. He was able to identify with people in a way that made them feel he loved and understood them—even people with very different social and moral backgrounds.

Facing this problem of judgment as a Christian helper is very important in loving people in the world. When I first became a Christian, I remember feeling that I sure didn't want to be a do-gooder or ever to judge people or put them down. But on the other hand I wasn't about to admit that I had the same problems they did. "After all," I thought, "they'll lose respect for me and any loving help I have to offer." But one day in a counseling situation a man confessed a problem in a close relationship in his life which reflected some attitudes he definitely considered to be un-Christian. He was a very sensitive person, and his rejection of himself for having those feelings was intense. After his confession, I looked at him for a long minute; he seemed so lonely with his problem— and I was horrified to realize that I had had the *same difficulty that morning*. I was tempted to pray for him and keep still about my problem. Actually I just wanted to get away. But since we were in my office, I couldn't. I found myself sort of sheepishly telling the man in his misery that I had experienced the same kind of jealousy and hostile resentment *that same day*.

I thought he would walk out of my office in disgust. But instead, he just looked at me in disbelief and said, "Are you serious?" Then I really wished I hadn't told him. But when I nodded my head, he began to weep and said. "Oh, *thank* you. If you've got this problem and are able to keep going as a committed Christian, maybe I can. I have been so *alone*." I remember being surprised at his reaction and realizing that he hadn't primarily wanted an "answer man." He wanted someone to be *with him* in his problem. And my identification with him as a "sinner" was a kind of "answer" from his perspective—since far from being his judge, I was *side* by *side* with him before God in need of grace and forgiveness.

An Attitude of Identification

As time has gone on and I have experienced and confessed more of my own sins and failures, I can often "hear" and understand these same failures with empathy when I meet them in the lives of people I'm trying to help.

As I started getting more deeply involved with people's inner lives and heard about all kinds of sins and failures I thought just happened in books, I realized how protected I'd been. I wanted to listen and identify with people's sins, but I saw that I couldn't honestly imply I'd been places and done things I hadn't.

And since I have not committed every sin nor failed in every way, I wondered how I could relate to problems I've never experienced. The late Gordon Allport helped me with this. He pointed out that we can learn to respect people as persons and identify with them by an imaginative extending of our own rougher experiences in the direction of the problems we encounter. For instance, I may never have stolen $100,000, but I can remember stealing a stapler from a major oil company over twenty-five years ago when I was starting my business career. The uneasiness, the rationalizations—I can extend all the feelings in my own imagination and understand "another" thief much better. As a matter of fact, as I look back I can see that I have not encounterd any sins or failures in other people which I could not imagine myself being involved in to some extent under some circumstances.

And I think that is the key to the most helpful attitude for a Christian lover in producing creative change in the world—to realize that in some way we can walk in almost anyone's shoes—as God did in ours—in order to learn to respect them and identify with them in the midst of their sins and stupid mistakes, which in God's eyes evidently aren't much different from ours. And because *we* are personally experiencing the healing forgiveness of God and have this to bring to others, we have a way to help which can lead to deep and lasting changes in their total lives.

The Attitude of Taking Confession Seriously

I remember one Christian woman who came to me some years ago at a weekend retreat. In great horror she told me that she had committed adultery after years of being faithful to her husband. And since she was a pillar in her church, this had made her feel especially terrible. I listened quietly and felt the pain the woman was describing. She had gone to a psychiatrist who had told her she really hadn't done anything wrong, that times had changed, and that she should just dismiss her adultery as something that was ill advised and go on.

But she said to me, "Keith, I *know* that I have sinned. Don't you think what I did was *terrible?*"

I looked at her and said, "Yes, I really do. I think according to your own standards it was probably the worst thing you could have done. You have *really* sinned!"

She looked surprised when I went on to say, "Isn't it great that God can only deal with us when we are aware of our sin—that he really wants to forgive us if we confess our sins!" Her surprise turned to relief. She began to shake her head and wipe the tears from her eyes. Finally she smiled, "Thank you for letting me have my sin and claim it," she said. And we prayed together and thanked God. When someone confesses while dealing with a problem I feel as if my job as a brother Christian is to listen, to feel that person's pain to the extent that I can, to receive his or her confession in Christ's name and point out that that's the place at which God helps us—when we see that we have in fact sinned. The realization of our forgiveness by God following a confession often gives us immediate and strong motivation to make lasting changes in our behavior and attitudes. And the memory of the agony of guilt and the subsequent release and gratitude are strong motivators to maintain the changed behaviors. But it seems to me that the attitude of honesty and non-judgmental understanding is one of the most effective ways to aid in this healing process.

For me this attitude of walking with people and listening creatively with a nonjudgmental but honest and responsible identification with them has allowed me to take part in more creative change than have all my advice and manipulations put together.

But there are certain destructive ideas and myths which are held by people who are helping and by those having difficulties which block their ability to ask for or receive help.

The Myths of a Stable Christian Life as a Block to Growth and Change

When I first began to hear evangelical teachers and writers, I used to be struck by the implication some of them seemed to make. "If we *really* give our lives to Jesus," they said, "and ask for the filling of his Spirit, then we will have a 'stable Christian life.'"

I tried to believe this, but if I were honest I had to admit that I had ups and downs—even after asking for the gift of the Holy Spirit. Then I felt guilty, as if I hadn't received as good a dose of the Holy Spirit as those speakers who implied that now they had very stable "up" lives all the time.

When I discovered that the stable life theory is very *unlike* the experience of the New Testament Christians, I was relieved. But I did find that it is very difficult to love and help people who believe that they shouldn't have ups and downs. And the knowledge of how this fallacy works has helped me in loving people in and out of the church who feel guilty about having problems in the first place.

Some of us Christians, for instance, often feel guilty if we don't have a constant desire for God. And when we have periods of great enthusiasm followed by lukewarmness we feel that our faith has failed and that we are in some kind of sinful condition. But it may only be that we are going through the normal spiritual and emotional fluctuations of the Christian life. In fact there is scarcely any such thing as a "stable spiritual life" if people are growing and facing the normal changes of living.

Many people think that they have "lost the victory" when they sin specifically (especially after having been filled with the Holy Spirit). But this is a great misunderstanding. The emotional "victory" that people claim simply does not exist. Christ has the victory, as I understand it, and though we share his victory, we will always have certain fluctuations in our feelings because of the way we are made. The necessity for constant victory would be like saying, "I didn't have a good year this year because it wasn't spring the whole year round." The victory mentality assumes that the rest of life will be spring. And even a normal winter is enough to bring depression and defeat in that kind of thinking. So people who feel that they are inadequate because of normal doubts and emotional fluctuations are difficult to help until they see that their vacillating feelings are universal and healthy for good people—and even good Christians.

Conflict and Hostility Natural, but Often Misdirected

The first time I tried to help someone who turned on me in anger and sarcasm, I wanted to withdraw from the Christian loving business fast. I felt I had done nothing but try to help in a loving way, and the person blasted me and accused me of being a hypocrite and a self-righteous prig. And he had come to me for help. I was baffled and felt very rejected.

It wasn't until years later that I realized that every person we may try to love or help is almost sure to be carrying a certain amount of resentment and hostility. He or she may not be *conscious* of these things because society (and particularly *Christian* society) does not approve of hostility and resentment; in fact, we punish our children for having them. But many people who need help are often consciously or unconsciously angry at God and the people around them. They may have been laughed at in Sunday school or mistreated by a parent who claimed to be a Christian. And they may be mad at God about their present problems. After all, while a person is miserable and floundering, *everyone else* seems to be coping so well. "It's not fair," he or she cries out to God.

Rather than take responsibility for one's own failures or bad feelings, a great part of sin is to blame someone else. And so we aim our resentment at other people when we have difficulties. These repressed feelings of anger, of blame and guilt are often like prison bars behind which the mind gets locked and becomes unable to get on with life. This is often the situation of people we encounter when we go out to love the world.

People who need help are often so paralyzed by feelings of resentment and hostility that they cannot think clearly about their situation or hear ideas about constructive change. Since the attitude of hostility is often actually aimed at someone in the *past,* it is *very* necessary for the helper to realize that he may be "getting someone else's mail"—that the person's anger is misdirected at the helper. This is hard to realize when someone is spitting in *your* face. But the knowledge is crucial in helping some people.

When I realized how much hostility I had unconsciously been sitting on all my life I was ready to give up as a helper. (I'd always thought I was a kind and loving person because I'd repressed my hostile feelings so deeply.) And that raised a big question about my right to go with Christ into the world in any serious way.

The Myth That You Must Be Sinless to Help People Make Changes in Their Lives

How does a Christian have the courage to accept the call to help when he has not gotten his own life in total alignment with Christ? I've had to face this in an even more poignant way in the last three years. Right after I was divorced I wanted to run away and hide and forget all about being a Christian, and, in particular, about being a Christian writer and one who sometimes counsels other people about marriage. I considered going back into the oil business and withdrawing from speaking and writing about the Christian life. But then one day, as I reached an almost despairing point, it was as if I had the following dialogue with our Lord. He seemed to say to me, "What would you advise someone else in your situation to do, Keith, since you're a counselor?" I told him, in this fantasy, that I would tell someone else to confess that he had failed in his marriage and that he had sinned and to get up and hit a lick for Jesus Christ. It was as if God said to me, "Are you going to do that, Keith?" And I replied, "No, sir, I'm a special case."

It is sometimes easy to tell another person what he or she should do about his or her marriage, about his or her failure, about his or her sin, about his or her agony. But any helper would do well to remember that it is very difficult to have the courage to confess, to receive *for yourself* the grace and forgiveness of God and go ahead living and helping.

But I realized that since "all have sinned and fallen short of the glory of God" (Rom. 3:23), he *must* use sinners to help. Some Christians seem to believe that there are certain failures for which there are no forgiveness and grace. But fortunately the God of the Bible doesn't seem to work that way.

Our authority for helping is not our righteousness in any case. We will never have totally stable lives nor be completely free of hostility and conflict or be sinless. Our authority, our calling, and the power we bring as sensitive helpers to the helping situation all come through the forgiving Word and the Spirit of God. On this attitude we must bet our lives. Since no sin, no problem, no difficulty is too great for our Lord to meet in love, we do not have to be afraid to find out the truth about ourselves, our inadequacies, our mixed motives, and the motives of those we meet who also need God's help to change their hopeless situations. And since there is always forgiveness, then, as Jesus said, in one sense the bigger the sin or failure that is forgiven, the greater the release and love that can follow (Luke 7:47). And for many people in despair who cannot love nor receive love that is good news indeed. It certainly is for me.

MEMORANDUM

TO: Bruce

FROM: Keith

RE: Chapter Four—Creative Change and What Produces It

Dear Bruce,

I'm seeing that even if I were perfectly motivated, helping people change their circumstances and their lives is not simple. As a matter of fact, a good many people are not sure we **can** do **anything** substantial to change our lives in a positive way. Will you say something about this? If it's not possible for people to decide to change things and do it, then the whole Christian helping venture is hamstrung before it begins.

Can people change radically? What's the function of the will in change? And how can we use our wills to bring about creative change? What are some of the reasons people change? And how can we handle changes which come in our lives as Christians— since it seems that we all have to face change whether we want to or not?

Bruce, I've been realizing that you've helped me more than almost anyone to be realistic about facing changes I needed to make in my life. I hope we can get together soon to talk about the implications of this book for our own futures.

Keith

One of my favorite scenes in the musical version of Charles Dickens' *Oliver Twist* is the one in which that old scoundrel Fagan sings "Can A Man Change?" It is a moment of high drama near the climax of the show, and it mirrors a universal yearning in all of us. Who has not been haunted by that question at a crossroad climax in life? Report card time! Can the grasshopper become a studious ant? Job scene! Can the procrastinator get out and sell? Marriage! Can the touchy, critical person become a friend and lover? Can the fat person ever be thin? The alcoholic, sober? The spendthrift, prudent? The clumsy, athletic? The depressed, happy? Choose your own area for contemplation—the question is the same. Can a person intentionally change? And any Christian setting out to help people must ask himself this question.

One thing is certain. If your answer to the question is an unqualified yes you are hopelessly naïve. On the other hand, an unqualified no comes only from a hardened cynic. Truth lies somewhere between yes and no.

Basic to the Christian faith, however, is a firm belief that people can change. "If any one is in Christ, he is a new creation" (2 Cor. 5:17, RSV). And if people can change intentionally then institutions can change, for they are, in essence, working groups of individuals.

Now let's examine some of the components of change: What changes and what does not? Why do some people and institutions change more easily than others? What can be done to facilitate change? These are important questions, for change is inevitable during all of life. For the living, change is as natural as the tides and the sunrise. Changelessness is synonymous with stagnation and death.

Changed Lives and Institutions

Experience confirms that people can change radically through personal commitments in their lives. Eldridge Cleaver and Malcolm Muggeridge are two of the more dramatic contemporary examples of this kind of change. I have witnessed any number of such radical transformations in the lives of friends and acquaintances over the

76

years. In some cases, they returned from a weekend conference so changed that they were practically unrecognizable to their coworkers on Monday morning. Inner changes took place that altered the way they looked, talked, walked, behaved. For some of these people change was necessary for survival, so desperate were their circumstances.

And institutions under great pressure must change to survive. Other institutions change so slowly that they appear to be standing still. Our educational institutions, for example, have undergone enormous change over the past hundred years or so, even though at any given time their critics might have felt they were locked into the status quo. To be convinced of this change, we need only to read something like the original requirements for South Hadley Seminary, now Mt. Holyoke College. Here are some of the standards which the founders of that school required of young ladies who applied for admission in those early days: "(1) Admission. No young lady shall become a member of this school who cannot kindle a fire, wash potatoes, and repeat the multiplication table. (2) Outfit. No cosmetics, perfumaries, or fancy soaps will be allowed on the premises. (3) Exercise. Every member of this school shall walk at least a mile every day unless a freshet, earthquake, or some other calamity prevents it. (4) Company. No member of this school is expected to have any male acquaintances unless they are retired missionaries or agents of some benevolent society. (5) Time at the mirror. No member of this institution shall tarry before the mirror more than three consecutive minutes. (6) Reading. No member of this school shall devote more than one hour each week to miscellaneous reading. *The Atlantic Monthly*, Shakespeare, Scott's novels, *Robinson Crusoe,* and immoral works are strictly forbidden. *The Boston Recorder, The Missionary Herald,* and Washington's farewell address are earnestly recommended for light reading." In the last half of the 20th century these antiquated requirements are merely laughable. But it's obvious that a whole lot of change has taken place, however imperceptibly.

On the other hand we have witnessed astonishing changes in our whole approach to education in just the past decade. We are moving away from authoritarian faculties into more and more cooperative faculty/student decision-making. Humanistic education is taking seriously the task of growing people rather than merely transmitting ideas. In this radical new approach, the teacher is seen as colearner. All of this has occurred in a few short years.

Tracing the Steps of Change

But how does all of this change actually come about? One of the great American psychologists, William James, was fascinated with the subject of change and with the religious conversion experience in particular. He contended that radical change was not only possible but could be documented in many lives. In an effort to discover the dynamics of change, James made a careful study of people who had experienced religious conversion. The results of his study and his revealing definition of religious conversion were published in 1902 in his book entitled *The Varieties of Religious Experience.* Here is his definition of radical change in terms of both behavior and identity: "To be converted . . . is a process, gradual or sudden, by which a self hitherto divided, and consciously wrong, inferior, and unhappy, becomes unified and consciously right, superior, and happy, in consequence of its firmer hold on religious realities."

After exhaustive research into the lives of many people who had been converted, James found a pattern emerging. "The steps leading up to the conversion experience are three-fold: effort, passivity, and surrender."

An example from everyday life (one, incidentally, which Viktor Frankl uses in logotherapy) can help us understand the pattern James describes. Most of us have had the frustrating experience of trying without success to recall a person's name. It is buried in your subconscious, and the harder you try to recall it, the more elusive it becomes. Finally, you give up . . . put it out of your mind . . . forget about it—you surrender. Then, when least expected, the elusive name bursts into your consciousness.

According to William James, there is an intriguing parallel here with Christian conversion. If you are pursuing an experience of God with your whole soul, as if you could "do it" if you expend enough effort, the odds are it will happen only when you give up, surrender, and quit trying. James is quick to add, however, that being able to explain the conversion experience psychologically does not account for the miraculous part God plays in it. To understand something about the experience does not mean you can duplicate the channels and methods by which God touches a life and brings about change.

Change and Positive Thinking

More recently, psychological pioneers have been reexamining the role of the will in change. Robert Assagioli, founder and developer of psychosynthesis in Italy, had this to say in an interview which appeared in *Psychology Today* just before his death: "I believe the will is the Cinderella of modern psychology. It has been relegated to the kitchen. The victorian notion that will power could overcome all obstacles was destroyed by Freud's discovery of unconscious motivation. But, unfortunately, this led modern psychology into a deterministic view of man as a bundle of competing forces with no center. This is contrary to every human being's direct experience of himself. At some point, perhaps in a crisis when danger threatens, an awakening occurs in which the individual discovers his will."

One technique Assagioli uses to develop will power is visualizing the "ideal model." You are asked how your life would be different if you were in possession of a strong will and asked to picture that goal as vividly as possible. And this simple process often enables people to act as their model would—even though they may still be afraid.

Another simple technique Dr. Assagioli used to empower the will was to place a series of cards around the room on which were printed evocative words such as *calm, patience, bliss, energy, good will.* He claimed that these printed words could trigger changed attitudes that call forth the quality they symbolize.

Assagioli's approach may seem simplistic, but I think he is rediscovering an age-old truth. Those who have denied the power of the will and have ridiculed the positive thinking approach of Coué or Norman Vincent Peale, may have to reexamine their conclusions. Psychologically it seems to be a valid and sound approach to bringing about certain important changes.

The Use of Positive Imagery to Bring about Change

Positive imagery in picturing an "ideal model" is a technique I have used personally over the years especially in intercessory prayer. For instance, I pray for the sick or the troubled while picturing them well and happy, full of strength and faith and God's own Spirit.

In the dynamic of group process, this "ideal-model" notion Assagioli speaks of can enable change. I've seen this work dramatically in many Christian groups. People have experienced God and been changed because of their desire to live up to the group's ideals. Thus, God can use the church as a family of believers to bring about personal change through positive modeling. God's most powerful witness to the world may very well be the small companies of his people who try to live in fellowship with one another in obedience to his will, visualizing a world and a group in which there is love and healing. Frequently, people who come in contact with such a group are drawn into it, and are consequently strengthened in their faith, led to a conversion experience or helped to face their problems and self-defeating behaviors—and to change.

Reasons to Change

Let's look now at some of the reasons for change, many of which are applicable to individuals as well as to groups of people. Tom Harris, the psychiatrist, speaks of three in his book *I'm OK—You're OK. First,* he says people change when it is more painful to remain as they are than to change. I made a major change in my life a few years back for just this reason. I left a job that had become my very life to strike out into a new dimension of work and ministry. It was terribly threatening and failure seemed imminent. But, under the circumstances, to remain would have been even more painful.

Business changes often come about in this way. Or sometimes the work scene may be comfortable but perhaps the product has become obsolete. Change is preferable to economic disaster. To stay with the old secure methods or products and resist change may spell failure.

A *second* reason for change, according to Tom Harris, emerges when we find ourselves at the point of despair. Change is an option, for instance, for the person suffering depression, or whose marriage is dissolving, or who really wants to be cured of his alcoholism. In fact, the rehabilitated alcoholic is a classic example of this kind of change. The alcoholic who has finally lost job, family, health, and even self-respect is ready to "try anything." It is at this point that he may call his AA friends or turn up at an AA meeting.

Finally, Harris believes that a *third* motive for change is brought about for individuals or organizations at the "eureka" stage—the moment of sudden discovery that there is a better way to live or act or relate. Saul's conversion following his Damascus Road experience is one such "eureka" experience. Suddenly Saul discovered that the God he had been fighting is in truth the one true and loving God. From that "eureka" moment, Saul, the man who was to become Paul, started the long process of training which would enable him ultimately to become God's ambassador to the gentiles.

It is this "eureka" kind of change which produced Martin Luther,

Augustine, and John Wesley, as well as the thousands of people in today's society who are discovering new truths about themselves, the world or God. And in business and the professions this "eureka" experience often is the starting point for new products, new markets, or new programs and techniques.

So in setting out to help people change, it is helpful to be able to recognize these three symptoms: the intense pain they may be experiencing, the point of despair, or the sudden and insightful moments out of which a new discovery might come to redirect a life.

Handling Inevitable Change

It seems to me that all of us experience two basic kinds of change: the *inevitable* and the *self-initiated.* Inevitable change occurs simply because we are alive. Friends die; we become ill; wars erupt; our children grow up, leave home, or disappoint us—all of life seems to be a series of disruptive and inevitable changes.

It's difficult enough to handle a positive kind of change that improves our lifestyle, but any change that might deprive us of what we hold dear is most dreaded and frightening. However, I believe there are surprising resources in most people of faith for handling inevitable change. Even people with no declared religious faith or conscious resources of strength somehow manage to handle the blows that life deals out. Surprisingly few break down emotionally or physically. Most come through with courage and resiliency.

Choosing Change

But the adventure of life comes as we are able more and more to embrace and welcome *self-initiated* change, as individual persons or as groups. Self-initiated change is that change which comes about as the result of choice. We can choose to risk and dare in relationships, in financial or vocational matters, or to help in causes that affect our neighborhood and world. I believe we need help with this kind of change—the kind of help available through personal relationships and small groups. We can encourage each other to be open to change, to have positive attitudes toward it, to become people who are able to change and to act as change agents for one another in society.

Abraham, the patriarch of the Old Testament, is one of our primary models for change. By *choice* he left his home and friends and business and country and culture and all the familiar surroundings of his life and began the search for what he believed was God's destiny for him and for the spiritual nation to follow. Change and uncertainty were his constant companions—by choice. Abraham has been called by the Bible "the father of the faithful." He models for us the ability to choose change in response to God's leading. He failed, he flinched, he doubted, he lied—but he also had faith and he never turned back.

Chapter Five

The Anatomy of
Change

MEMORANDUM

TO: Bruce

FROM: Keith

RE: Chapter Five—The Anatomy of Change

Dear Bruce,

In my discussion of some of the attitudes and ideas which affect the change process I didn't even mention a number of the forces, fears and levels of change which seem crucial in understanding the dynamics of changing.

How about discussing the anatomy of change from the perspective of the desire to help people? What keeps us from wanting to help others through the doorways which would lead to creative change? As potential helpers, how do we handle our own fear of change? Is the church helpful to those who want to change? What is different about us when we change (e.g., attitudes, knowledge, behavior)? And what about social change?

It's all yours!

Keith

P.S. Walking on the beach and eating Haze's wonderful shrimp dish on Saturday was great. I always feel all charged up and ready to work again after being with you all.

When we see that change for others is as frightening as it is for us, we begin to understand the challenge involved in being a helper.

It seems that God made each of us so unique that we defy any kind of neat classification in terms of the way we will choose to behave. Nevertheless I am convinced that there is a common powerful force operating in most of us and that is a *desire to help other people*. We may give an outward appearance of being totally selfish and egocentric, yet our imaginations are caught by characters such as Cervantes's Don Quixote, because he embodies for us our own hidden desire to be a rescuer and helper of people in distress or danger.

In the 1950s, J. D. Salinger's famous novel, *Catcher in the Rye,* spoke to this aspect of our character. His hero, Holden Caulfield, seems to be the typical adolescent, rebelling and reacting to his privileged prep-school-student role. But, confronted by his little sister late one night in her New York City bedroom, Holden shares with her what he really wants to be.

He describes a field of rye above a sheer cliff where little children are romping and playing joyfully. It seems that he wants to be the person standing near the cliff, so positioned that he can catch any child who might wander too close to the edge and fall over.

Who would have guessed that Salinger's rebellious teenage hero was a kindred soul to that senile old Spanish gentleman, Don Quixote? These two characters and a host of similar ones from literature speak to all of us because they bring to the surface our own deep longings to somehow count for good in the world. And we intuitively know that these yearnings draw us toward wholeness.

An Impediment to Helping: The Fear of Change

But what keeps us all from being catchers in the rye or modern-day knights out to do battle with the forces of evil? I'm inclined to feel that it is our fear that such action will require some drastic change in ourselves, our reputations or in our lifestyles. We may be thought naïve and rejected. We may get sidetracked from our competitive goals, and left behind. It seems likely that our passion to help conflicts with our fear of risk and change. To release the positive force within which urges me to be a helper of people, I must change my safe position and take a new and more vulnerable position toward life and the one who needs help. Further, those I feel moved to help may find their present predicament more comfortable than an unfamiliar new position, which may or may not be safe. And they may well reject my help. Our universal fear of change and rejection blocks all of us in our efforts to become priests and helpers.

Karl Marx once said, "If you want to understand the structure of the world, try to change it." This is true for people as well. In fact, I believe our attitudes toward change can be an accurate measure of our growth toward wholeness in Christ. If we are ready to risk changes on the adventure of life with Christ and some of his people, he will lead us to a place where we can help others to change and grow in knowledge of life and of God. But far too many of us are locked into set patterns of thinking and living. We resist change vigorously, satisfied with the comfortable rigidity of our stale routines. And this resistance blocks our relationship with our Lord, who is always out ahead calling us to adventure with him.

And yet we know that life is movement, not a static position. To live in Christ is to act . . . to do . . . to be! Inactivity produces atrophy, stagnation, and death. Medically speaking, increased movement and activity are often signs that the patient is on the way to recovery.

To me the very heart of the nature of God is that he is a fountainhead of change. It is true that he is an unchanging God whose nature and purpose are stable. But as he interacts with the world in the dynamics of change he is always bringing forth a new thing, guiding and leading those who believe in him and respond to him. In fact, the unchanging God is in some sense the initiator of all change.

The Church Can Block Change

But, tragically, far too often the Christian church has been a powerful change-resistant agent. The gospel has sometimes been used to fight change and to protect the status quo. The Bible has been cited as a defense for slavery and an excuse for the second-class status of women. It has been quoted to justify those opposing scientific advances of all sorts. What a perversion of God's true nature and plan. It seems to me that to understand the church as the people of God, we need to understand God's purpose for us as found in Isaiah 43:18–19: "Cease to dwell on days gone by and to brood over past history. Here and now I will do a new thing; this moment it will break from the bud. Can you not perceive it?" (NEB).

Paradoxically, even the most adventuresome of us still fear change. As I mentioned earlier, people who have been faced with freezing to death tell us they experience a cozy, warm feeling that seduces them into inactivity. To survive, a person must shake off this comfortable feeling, move his arms and legs and change positions frequently. To stay alive during long exposure to freezing conditions, one must not succumb to instinctive feelings. But movement is every bit as essential to our mental and spiritual life. We must help each other shake off the comfortable feelings that lead to death. To stay as we are, to think the way we always have and to act in old patterns is nonthreatening and comfortable, but it lulls us toward a frightening death of the soul. To stay alive we must be people on the move, alert to the exciting opportunities of change.

Four Levels of Change

As we get involved in helping people, we find many of them are struggling with change and their fear of change. It's helpful to understand something of how and why change is actually brought about. At a University of Massachusetts seminar, Ken Blanchard, one of the school's professors, talked about four distinct kinds of change. The *first* he terms a *knowledge* change. We change because we come to know more about a person, subject, situation, approach, or strategy.

Second, there is *attitudinal* change. This level of change involves the emotions. People feel strongly about a certain position, precept, or approach, and they resist change because of these attitudes.

The *third* level of change is *behavioral* change. This means that in spite of how we feel, in spite of our fears, reluctance, or doubts, we try to change our behavior. And as difficult as behavioral change is, in my opinion, it is less difficult than attitudinal change. Perhaps this is because we have less control over our emotions, feelings, and attitudes than we do over our behavior.

If we can start with behavioral changes—*do* something differently, approach a problem with more integrity, perform deliberate acts to express love and concern—perhaps an attitudinal change will result. There is actually strong psychological and historical evidence which indicates that when behavior changes, attitudes eventually change. So we can often help people to change their *behaviors* when they are stuck at the *attitudinal* level.

The *fourth* level of change that Blanchard mentioned was *organizational* change—a change in group behavior. When a familiar organization to which we belong, such as a church, civic group, union, social or service club, decides to change its rules, goals, membership, or financial policies, it is usually upsetting to those of us who did not initiate the change. Most of us derive a great deal of security from the groups we belong to, and any attempt to change those groups represents a threat to our security pattern and our way of life. Renewal programs in the church have often run into resistance for this very reason.

It seems to me that Blanchard is saying something very helpful to anyone who is working for change in a particular situation. By using any or all of these four strategies, people may be enlisted and harnessed to help others.

One of my dearest friends was a retired clothing manufacturer in Pennsylvania named Sam Elkins, a member of a large and prestigious Presbyterian church. At a lay renewal conference in New York City, Sam met a man who was then heading up a unique Christian ministry on the Lower East Side of New York. They were trying to demonstrate an alternative way of life to street kids, their parents, and other adults. Sam was grabbed by the desperate needs of the people in this area and by the hope this new ministry represented. Although his church was about one hundred miles away, he wanted to use some of their abundant resources and talents to make a difference in the lives of these people in the ghetto.

He began by getting some of the leaders to come out and talk to groups in his church. Their powerful communication brought knowledge about what life was like for kids growing up on New York's Lower East Side and motivated some to join Sam in his desire to help. This first group of allies experienced, in Blanchard's terms, a *knowledge* change.

Next, this newly formed group arranged a series of visits in which teenagers and adults from the inner-city area could spend the weekend in the homes of church members. Soon dozens of families developed good friends who lived in the needy section of New York. Former negative *attitudes* about people in these circumstances (e.g., that they are lazy, irresponsible and content to receive welfare) began to change.

About a year later, this growing group of concerned suburbanites took part in a four-day renewal conference on the Lower East Side. About fifty affluent, middle-aged church members actually traveled into New York and were housed with ghetto families. This was the beginning of many such visits and this new *behavior* eventually resulted in a mighty flood of concern and help.

Eventually this Lower East Side ministry became an official part of the outreach program in my friend's church. New members were immediately confronted with the opportunity to help in this ministry. Change was effected at the *institutional* level. My friend Sam had begun and enlarged this crosscultural cooperation by bringing about change on all four of the levels explored by Blanchard.

Individual and Social Change

The Christian church has traditionally been divided as to the best means of bringing about change on a major scale. For years, one voice of Christendom said that changed laws and changed institutions can only come about through changed individuals. "You can't make a good omelet out of bad eggs." At the other pole, equally Christian voices were saying, "Your approach doesn't work! Look at history. We can't wait for changed individuals to change society." They then proceeded to try to bring about legislation and changed laws through all kinds of demonstrations, coercion, and legal maneuvering. Their belief was that a new society would in turn bring about new individuals.

I don't believe any of us have the luxury of choosing one or the other approach. Changed people do become a leaven for a new society. But a new society, we have discovered in recent history, can begin to change the people in it—even their deepest prejudices and doubts.

We'll discuss approaches to instigating and implementing specific kinds of social changes in subsequent chapters.

I remember a dinner party some years ago at which I heard a public health nurse from Canada talking about her work among the Eskimos. She said that before the arrival of the white man these people had not had serious mental or emotional problems, but now many of them were experiencing anxiety neurosis.

A doctor sitting next to me exploded joyfully, "That's wonderful! It's about time they joined the human race!"

We were all a little stunned to think he was glad about the Eskimos' new pain. But on reflection, I think he was saying he was glad for their new awareness. The doctor knew that all peoples who are aware of what's going on in the modern world will share in its anxiety to some extent. Without this awareness very little creative change can take place. And in our attempts to help people we may trigger resistance and fears. But these dynamics of creative change, though painful and sometimes frightening, are also signs of life and hope.

MEMORANDUM

TO: Keith

FROM: Bruce

RE: Chapter Five—The Anatomy of Change

Dear Keith,

The topic for this chapter is tailor-made for you.

You mentioned once that in your adult life, you have moved nineteen times in something like thirty years. That means that you've had to deal with an awful lot of decisions about change.

With that in mind, I hope you will take our readers through all the stages we go through in making these life-changing decisions.

There were porpoises in the canal today. I love those creatures. They always remind me of the quality of life God can give us— abandoned joy.

Bruce

The Forces at Work to Produce Change

Making decisions to change jobs or to go back to school, to get married, to decide to become a full-time writer, to face the possibility of divorce, to move to another part of the country—these and other decisions involving serious changes in my life have provided some of the most agonizing hours I could have imagined. I have been so afraid of failure and of the disapproval of people I love that decisions to change have been especially fearful to me. "What if I'm making a mistake?" I wonder. "What if I'm just being selfish and dumb?"

To compensate for these fears I have moved my residence nineteen times in thirty years as an adult. And at last I am beginning to see a pattern or process in the making of decisions to change.

I've found very little written about what people go through when they are considering an important change in their lives. But if we're trying to love people in trouble and help them to make healthy creative adjustments toward wholeness, it seems important to know all we can about the anatomy of the change process. So I'm going to try to present here a "picture" of the process of making a decision to change. Naturally it would be dangerous to generalize completely from the model of the anatomy of change I'm going to present. It will not fit in all cases nor in all aspects of any one case. But I'm hoping that through this rough description, you may identify with the feelings and the struggles that arise when people are going through a crisis of change.

Let's say for an example, that we are talking about considering a change in vocation. My own experience over the years would indicate that a similar process would be true with regard to a change in schools, perhaps a change of majors within a school, a change of denominations, or even a change in marital status. And although we are dealing in this chapter with individual change, we believe that the principles and many of the steps also apply to whole groups of people as well, like those who are attempting to bring about racial equality, a change in the status of women, or a remedy for a deteriorating neighborhood.

92

An Example of the Process of Deciding to Make a Change

Of the several very traumatic moves in my own vocational life, one that took place when I was attending graduate theological seminary seems to offer the most insight into the anatomy of change.

I had been in the oil exploration business for two years but was very restless. I kept being plagued by questions about what I should do with my life. Perhaps because of having buried almost all of the people I'd grown up with by the time I was twenty, I had a lot of questions about life and death and God. Through a series of "chance" meetings and discoveries I finally decided to go to seminary—that that was God's will for my life—even though I had not yet tried to commit my whole future to him. Going to seminary seemed to be what God would have me do. And because I wanted to learn all I could about him and the meaning of life, the decision was not too traumatic. So I went off to seminary with a wife and baby.

After some months, a change began to take place. I had given up a good job, gone 1,700 miles with very little in the way of financial support, and had been in seminary for four terms. My father had not been a religious man and didn't respect most professionals in that field so I felt he would not have approved. I wanted to learn about God but couldn't picture myself in the priestly robes. After a term I had thought about leaving, but I had never liked to see myself as a quitter. Besides, I had left the oil business to go to seminary. What would my friends think—who already thought I was strange for leaving the business world? What should I do?

Finally after four terms, I began to have strong feelings that I was in the wrong place. And yet how could I make a decision which might seem to be against God's will? Such a decision would make me look like the foolish and indecisive boy I felt I must be. Before I knew it I was in the pit of hell trying to decide whether to leave the seminary.

As I look back, I can see that there were definite stages I went through while considering whether to leave or stay. Those stages I now believe apply to many life-changing decisions.

Restlessness

First there was a vague *restlessness*. Something seemed to be wrong with my being a priest. I had wanted to learn but had not felt called to be ordained. But the only way I could get into the seminary had been to go as a postulant for holy orders. I'd been honest with the bishop, and he'd said that many people went to seminary with those feelings and that by going I'd find out whether or not I wanted to be ordained. But when I got there everyone just assumed that I was going on into the ministry.

Though I loved the studies I could not get over the uneasiness I felt about becoming a priest. I began to feel a vague dissatisfaction with the classes, the teachers, the students. This dissatisfaction blossomed into an intense desire to leave. I began to get headaches when I tried to study and developed an acid stomach when I thought about my situation. I told myself I was being immature. But after a few weeks I began to have trouble sleeping and was irritable with my family.

Fantasizing the Change and "Building a Case"

The second stage began when I started actually *fantasizing* being back in the business world. While driving to school or in the midst of a class I'd imagine being back in business, laughing and enjoying my old friends, or being in an exotic new place and with a different cast of characters. And I felt much better as I imagined myself in the familiar role of an "oil man." This was, I learned later, the *approach* phase of changing. And it included some pretty happy fantasies of what life would be "if only . . ." I imagined being peaceful and happy, and I repressed all the unpleasant things about working in the oil business. I began to pray for release to make the change. This just magnified my dissatisfaction with the seminary. And I began to look for and find faults where there had been none—picking at things I hadn't considered serious before I began to think seriously about leaving.

I now call this "building a case." We build a case against our present job, denomination, or wife or husband we'd like to leave. Building a case against the seminary added all kinds of fuel to the fire I had in my imagination about leaving. Finally, when the idea of staying became almost unbearable, I progressed from imagining making the change at the level of fantasy to considering specific steps I might take to make the change in the real world—actually leaving seminary and going back into the oil business. But as the approach feelings got strong enough for me to consider really making the move, a second curve began to appear on the graph—the *resistance* to changing.[1]

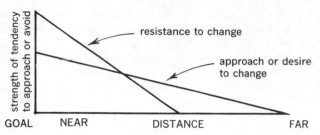

Resistance to Changing

This resistance made itself felt as a *fear* of changing. I began to imagine myself not being able to get a job in the oil business and failing to make a living. I'd visualize my wife and babies in want or need. Or I'd imagine my mother trying to explain to her friends that I'd quit the seminary and see their faces nodding as if they had always known I didn't have any courage or tenacity. I began to imagine God's disapproval of me for not "sticking it out—regardless of how unpleasant it might be." I remembered selective biblical admonitions to the effect that "once one puts his hand to the plow he should never turn back," etc. And the fear of leaving seminary began to gather strength. At that point I tried to get "back to normal" at school and tried to put myself fully into studying.

The fantasizing one does during the resistance phase is often enough to stop the change process. The vivid memories of past failures, rejections, or admonitions provide enormous barriers to making decisions to change one's life situation substantially. And the fear of change was almost enough to drive me back and make me satisfied to stay in school—but not quite.

The Struggle

I tried to forget that I felt like a misfit as a postulant for holy orders. I prayed. I begged God to make me want to stay since I assumed staying was God's will. And I walked for long hours through the city alone. But finally one day I realized that leaving was crucial to my hope for any peace of mind in the future. So I began to investigate further. At that point I asked myself very seriously, "Is this change *really God's* will for me?" But it didn't seem possible at that time that *leaving seminary* could be God's will—though I knew it wasn't right for me. I wasn't sure how one determined God's will and hadn't yet learned how a committed Christian learns to look through the lens of the Scriptures, the perspective of his Christian friends in a small group, and through meditation and prayer. But I discovered right then that when there is some doubt that a course a Christian is considering is God's will, it's possible to "send the Lord on vacation" while the decision is being investigated further. And I pushed God away and began to scramble on my own to figure out what to do. I still prayed, but mostly just to "help me to decide."

This point is the place at which many people need help—while they are still investigating the possibility of changing but have seemingly unanswerable questions. I went to a counselor. But he—wisely—refused to give me advice. I listed on one side of a piece of paper the reasons *for* making the change and on the back side the reasons *against* changing. This brought the various forces involved in the decision into focus, and getting them on paper objectified them. As is often true, there were about eight reasons to stay and only three to go. Sometimes this listing procedure will make the decision obvious. But I began to get frantic because I felt a strong seemingly irrational desire to leave in the face of all the reasons I "should" remain in school. I tried to want to stay, to reason with myself. But one of the things I'd written on the reasons-to-leave sheet was "you *must* go!"

It is difficult for some people to realize that many important decisions are often *not* made rationally. But the "right thing" is often seen as the thing the people around us think we should do. We decide a lot of questions at an unconscious level and seek frantically for logical reasons to show that we are "doing the right thing." For this reason, when we cannot rationalize our decisions to change *according to the values of the people around us* the struggle to make the decision is much more severe—and confusing.

At about that time an incident took place which made me realize I'd never be happy staying: a professor seemed to be making fun of my approach to faith. At that point the agony became excruciating. I knew beyond a doubt that I had to leave. But I could not. I was frantically thinking about how I could leave and still not feel guilty night and day. I got very haggard and was afraid I might be about to crack up—until finally one day staying didn't seem worth it, whatever the cost. But I still couldn't bring myself to act.

The Impasse

At that point the struggle changed. Now I began to worry about emotional survival. I started to sweat, to be anxious almost continually, and I lost any perspective I'd had. It seemed that a fog had come over my ability to decide anything intelligently.

My prayer life became frantic, and I found myself praying ineffectively for "the answer" all the time. I asked God to show me what I really wanted. Finally when the strength of the *resistance* to change equaled the strength of the *desire* to change, I was stuck with two equal but opposing needs and was in effect paralyzed. (See graph on p. 95.)

Most people do not let the agony get this intense. Before they get stuck, the fear of the effect of the continuing agony will drive them to decide one way or the other. But in the model I have chosen to present, trying to make a decision pushed me almost to the limit of my ability to cope. And my counseling experience would indicate that many people, particularly people with highly sensitized consciences and an intense need to be right, do get to a real impasse like the one described here.

At this "stuck point" one may become irrational, and sort of panicky. I certainly did. I began to fear that I would *never* be able to resolve my dilemma and that I would spend the rest of my life in that very agonizing situation unless I was released by having a nervous breakdown.

Since I couldn't bring myself to go against what seemed right to the people around me and yet I couldn't find any peace in staying, I stayed in a frantic and depressed state of indecision for several weeks. Finally one day I just realized that I really wanted only to leave, that I had to go whether anyone else thought I should or whether anyone ever approved of me again or not. I had to go! And with an enormous effort I made the decision and left.

Working toward a Decision*

The process of helping a person make a change like the one just described often begins by trying to find out what he really wants

---

* For the purpose of simplicity of language in the following section I will assume the person being helped to make a decision is an adult man. But the same considerations would apply in the case of a woman or young person.

to do. You may do this with some mechanical things like listing options or letting him free-associate and find the feasible alternative courses that he might take. But as long as he is hiding from himself what he wants to do, it's not possible for him to make a clear choice.

In my situation my need to be a "fine Christian man" was so great that for months I repressed the fact that I did not want to be a parish priest. Since the values of the faculty members and other students surrounding me seemed to indicate that God's will could only be to stay, I was afraid to admit even to myself how sincerely I wanted to leave. Only later did I see my true feelings and understand that God could use that decision to lead me to a place I described in Chapter One at which I could consciously try to commit my whole life to him. The point here is that the counselor's job is not to play God and tell another what God's will is for him, but rather to help him hear his true feelings and make a decision he can live with in integrity.

On the other hand you may realize that the struggler is aware that he really needs to make a change and that he has a definite decision in mind to make but just doesn't have the courage to make it.

When you listen to the person needing help, it is important to listen for strengths in his character, for abilities he has which will probably be revealed by what he says in telling his story. For instance, although he may feel totally helpless, the fact that he had the guts to seek help—if he has—is a positive sign. His having done a good bit of rather careful thinking and reasoning is a good sign. The fact that he has the ego strength to even consider making a change in the face of failure or censure is another good sign. Later, when you try to help him implement whatever decision he comes to, it may be extremely helpful to be able to remind him that he very likely has the strength to make it because of the characteristics he's revealed to you and because, in fact, he has made the decisions leading up to his change.

But let's say you have talked to this person in trying to help him and have realized that he really does want to make the change.

At any point in this process the person may suddenly become starkly aware that however good the change might be, in his case he will not have the strength to make it. Deciding to change would be going against some taboo or religious law that he simply cannot break—for instance, leaving the ministry or getting a divorce. He may back off and get to work in his present situation, deciding that he actually should be where he is and, in fact, that it is the only place for him to be. In that case he may come back to his present situation with a totally new attitude and become successful and creative in his approach to his life and work. He has solved the problem by receiving a new attitude rather than by changing his surroundings. His restless symptoms may disappear and he quite likely will become happy in his work.

On the other hand he may go back to work as I did only to realize he cannot change his attitude through any effort or prayer, and suddenly he is more miserable than ever. His physical and emotional symptoms may become intense, as I described. Since he has decided that he cannot make the change, his situation seems doubly hopeless. And he really begins to panic.

I knew of one woman who saw her vocation as marriage. After sixteen years she became terribly restless and wanted to get a divorce. But she had never failed in anything and had always been a "good girl." And she could not imagine herself failing. Her parents had been so proud of her, and everyone had affirmed her for not making mistakes. The idea of getting a divorce was totally abhorrent. Divorce indicated a despicable failure in the eyes of all the people she loved most—including God. But her whole mind and body began to scream at her that she was in the wrong marriage. She had unbelievable headaches and insomnia. Finally this woman got at the stuck point, and stayed there for *nine years,* unable to do anything. She spent most of her time in tears, could hardly relate to her family, and was hospitalized several times for emotional difficulties.

I call this kind of behavior the "white-knight syndrome"; that is, someone has such a fear of other people's opinion that he or she cannot decide to do anything that would lead to failure in the eyes of other people, thus failing to be the totally pure and totally adequate "white knight" or "princess" of the fairytales.

A Way Out of the Impasse

There are not very many ways out of this situation. Some people try suicide, since it seems impossible to break their taboo. Others begin unconsciously to sabotage their present situation and force change to be instigated by other people—change which they haven't got the courage to make directly themselves. In industry this often works, in that if one quits doing his work or starts getting drunk on the job, he may get fired and will therefore manage to avoid the responsibility of making his own decision to change. Of course, one may ruin his chance for another job by his irresponsible behavior; but since it is unconscious, he "can't help it." In a marriage, one can begin to be flagrantly unfaithful, drink too much, be abusive to one's mate in ways that pressure him or her toward divorce, thus effecting the desired change without ever having to take responsible action. This sabotaging often leads to an enormous amount of guilt and feelings of lack of worth (even though it is unconscious), and it is not an effective way to make changes. But it continues to happen since it sometimes does get the job done when all conscious routes seem impossible.

But let's say that the person in the dilemma really needs and wants to make a decision, and we as helper sense that the reason he can't is the enormous risk of failure or of displeasing an unreasonable external standard or parent.

If someone asks for help at this point, he may be drawn on toward a change by helping to sort out all the options "out there" as I suggested. But the chances are he will have to wait until the intensity of the struggle is so great that it is almost intolerable.

In the struggle of my deciding whether or not to leave seminary, I finally began to listen to my body. I was about to get ulcers and was extremely anxious all the time, could hardly sleep and was having trouble concentrating at all. Eventually the day came when I realized that I felt going was a matter of saving my sanity.

I am not saying that one should always follow the apparent advice of his body over his mind. But when these sorts of physical symptoms will not go away, it sometimes indicates that at a very primal level one's psyche is screaming at him that he is in the wrong place. If he tries to meet the present demands and cannot, he may have to leave in spite of the prohibitions, even if it seems totally "wrong" to do so by the standards of right and wrong around him.

Making One's Own Decision to Change

In helping someone, care must ordinarily be taken *not* to urge a decision in one direction or the other. If things work out badly, the one being helped may hate you and blame you. Or if things work out well, he may not feel as if he made the decision himself and may not have the ego strength to follow through in his new situation. Either way, he will have failed to take responsibility for his own life under God. So sometimes the helper has to wait and listen and watch while the person he is trying to help suffers. It is very difficult for me to stand by and let people at this stage suffer, but I have discovered that this is often very productive suffering. And if a person can make his own decision through prayer and with your help, the experience may change the rest of his life and teach him how to make future decisions on his own.

After the Change

After a person makes the decision, there may be an enormous relief, a period of joy and peace, of well-being, a sense of resolution, a feeling that all is right with the world, and a wondering how one could have waited so long to make a decision which now seems obvious.

Post-Decision Panic

On the other hand, some people may panic shortly after having made a decision. I usually ask them if the *situation itself* has changed. Are the reasons they decided to change positions still the same? If they are, then I remind them that nothing has changed except their feelings and they still have the same deep underlying reasons to leave. What is attacking them now are often irrational fears of the future. If they go back because of this fear only, they may be in a worse spot than before. And often it is much harder to get past the stuck point the second time than the first.

If people can only wait a few days or weeks after a change and begin to do constructive and specific things in their new situation, asking God to give them the strength to get through one day (or sometimes one hour) at a time they may be able to overcome their post-decision panic and move into a new chapter of their lives, or at least have a more objective view of their decision.*

Change Is a Process

In helping an individual or a group, it is valuable to realize that you may make your initial contact with them anywhere in the process just described. Where they are in the process determines what kind

---

* Of course, it is always true that someone could have made a real error and only know it after the fact. In such cases he may or may not be able to go back to his old situation. But at least he may be able to learn a great deal through his mistake.

of help they need or can receive. For instance, if they are in the stage of fantasizing the wonders of making a change, they may not even be able to hear questions about the possible dangers and fears they will face. But if they are in the stage of facing the resistances to changing, they may have temporarily forgotten the very valid reasons *for* moving. So it is always good to listen and try to see where people are with regard to the anatomy of change.

Finally, as Christian helpers, we can take a lot more chances than non-Christians. We believe that God can redeem any mistake and also that we are all going to sin and make mistakes continually. That is why we need grace and the Holy Spirit to forgive us again and again and give us new beginnings. We try not to fail, and we certainly don't encourage people to sin. But we don't have to panic when we or they do, because as Christians we can begin again with a clean slate and learn by adjusting to the mistakes we make.

Sometimes even when someone decides to do something I think is immoral or very bad for them, I believe it is better to go ahead and stay in a helping relationship with them, since there may be no other way they can learn about themselves, about life, and about God's will. The thing they need to hear, if and when they fail, is that God still loves them and can forgive them, even for bad mistakes. This somehow is much more therapeutic and healing in the long run than stopping them from doing something they feel they must do and having them blame you and not grow either. Besides, I think over the long haul—as threatening as it is to say—God is more interested in his children's total development than he is in keeping our noses absolutely clean, as we face the needs to grow and change.

Chapter Six

A Place to Begin

MEMORANDUM

TO: Bruce

FROM: Keith

RE: Chapter Six—A Place to Begin

Dear Bruce,

It seems to me that one of the most difficult problems I've faced with regard to understanding what I can do to help is to believe that my natural inclinations to help in a certain way can be trusted. In other words, if I think I'd **enjoy** helping in a particular way, then I suspect it **couldn't** lead to much "real Christian help." After all **Christian** helping should be costly and grim. Right? Wrong?

Why don't you discuss the whole business of helping in line with our natural inclinations? But there are some other questions people keep asking me regarding helping: Does God always prepare us if he calls us to help? To what extent does our pain help us to determine the scene of our helping? How can we support people in reproducing the help we give them? And finally, when do we just allow people to fail rather than rescue them?

I hope you're getting some warm weather. It's colder here than it has been in years. The Dallas Airport was even iced in! But that makes it easier to stay in and write.

Keith

Since my conversion to Jesus Christ during World War II, I have had a number of subsequent "conversions." One of them, as I suggested earlier, centered in my own need and pattern for helping.

But I am making some progress in the matter of impulsively rushing forth to fix things for people. Recently I received a long-distance call from a friend I had met at a conference. She suggested that I visit her brother who also lives in a Florida community, about one hundred fifty miles from our home. It seems that the brother was seriously ill and also suffered from many problems with himself, his family, and with God. My friend thought I could "help him a lot" with his problems and suggested that I go visit him.

Now, there was a time when I would have dropped everything without further thought and gone to see him. Instead, I explained to my distraught friend that I no longer initiate a relationship of this sort on someone else's guidance. If her brother would call or write, I would respond immediately. Experience has taught me that efforts of help not directly and personally asked for are often construed as a violation of a person's privacy and freedom of choice. For this reason I resist the temptation to play Mr. Fixit in the life of a third party who hasn't asked me directly for help and who may have very good reasons to resent my help. Believe me, I'm trying to curb my instinctive pattern of trying to play God and be the rescuer in an unhealthy way.

Learn How to Be Yourself as a Helper

I read a fascinating interview with the director of the movie *Oh, God*. He discussed some of the problems they had in directing George Burns in the lead role. It seems that George kept trying to act and talk as he assumed God would. They had to keep telling him, "George, don't be God, be George Burns. That's the whole point of the movie. God became George Burns." I'm convinced God doesn't want me to try to play God either. Rather, he wants me to be Bruce Larson, and Bruce Larson does not have unlimited time and resources and he doesn't have answers for everybody.

105

These days when I am called on for help, I find myself offering up flash prayers asking, "Lord, is this something you want me to do?"

Sometimes it seems right to say, "I'm sorry, but that doesn't appear to me to have my name on it. I think you're asking me to do something that God has told you to do instead." And frequently people who were at first shocked by that refusal have told me later how encouraged they felt because I believed they could solve a difficult problem alone or that they could help some third party in a sticky situation.

Helping Where Your Heart Dictates

But how do we sort out the thing that God *would* have us do—and the place to begin? We referred earlier to the fact that most of us have a strategy for helping other people as a result of our early conditioning which is reinforced by our own psychological needs. But our emotions are also good barometers sometimes in this business of deciding on the cause or concern which has our name on it. What problems or concerns distress you or outrage you the most? . . . a story about child abuse? . . . reports of substandard housing for senior citizens or minorities? . . . inadequate hospital care or the shortage of mental hospital facilities? . . . young people in trouble with the police or on drugs? It is possible that we may not even understand why a particular area of need grabs us, but the important thing is to believe that God has programmed us to respond to some situations more than others—consequently we may be more effective in helping there than anywhere else.

It's just possible that a story about a battered child got a special response from you because you were a battered child, or knew one. But, irrespective of the reason, your heart may be able to tell you strategies you can best employ to help. For one thing, you might spend time in the hospital as a nurse's aid working with these children and loving them back to health. If the parents live in your town, you might call them and offer to assist them in any way you can. You might even organize a television campaign about child abuse in your town and alert parents to danger signals. And if you have political knowhow, you might work to get laws passed which make a counseling program mandatory for parents of battered children. Obviously you can't do all of these things, but I believe there may be a piece of a problem for which God has equipped you uniquely to give relevant help.

Helping in Response to God's Call

We are not always limited to those areas where we seem prepared by training or experience to help. There may be occasions where God directs us to become a part of his love for the world in an area where we have no expertise at all. Many examples from history come to mind. The story of William Wilberforce in nineteenth-century England is such a drama. Wilberforce, a tiny hunchback, was not a slave, did not own slaves, and had very little experience with slaves. But he fought for forty years to abolish slavery in the British Empire. For some reason God used him as a key person in liberating millions of black people long before America's Emancipation Proclamation in 1863. Such examples illustrate how important it is to be open to this kind of divine mandate, a burning bush out of which God says, as he did to Moses, "You go."

Helping Where We Are

But usually we find the place that has our name on it by much more natural means. We are drawn to help in those areas where we have lived and suffered and where we have had a significant amount of involvement. Dried-up drunks help alcoholics. Overweight people are helped by those who have been overweight and are licking the problem. People on drugs are helped by former addicts through Narcotics Anonymous type programs. The list goes on and on.

An old friend, Bea Decker, lost her husband a number of years ago. She was very lonely. At the time she started a small group for other widows who were as lonely as she was. That ministry has now grown to such an extent that there are groups in dozens of states all over the country. The movement is called THEOS, and the initials stand for To Help Each Other Spiritually. It all began because one Christian woman found a way of dealing with her own grief constructively and reached out to others with similar problems.

The two women who organized the courageous group in Northern Ireland called The Mother's March for Peace began that movement when each of them lost loved ones in the bitter fighting. Friends of mine who live in that tormented land tell me it's the most helpful and hopeful movement on the horizon. But it was initiated by two housewives who were caught in the pain and hurt of their own grief.

Another marvelous movement in our time was started by Maggie Kuhn when she was in her seventies. She began a ministry to organize senior citizens with this letter:

> Dear Friend, to get to the airport from my home in Philadelphia I have to pass a junkyard, where old cars are thrown on a heap, left to rust and disintegrate, and finally smashed to smithereens by a society that wants everything shiny new. That junkyard haunts me because America does the same thing to people. When we turn sixty-five, we are trash. Well, I am seventy-one and I don't want to be dumped on the scrap heap. I don't want to be isolated from mainstream living or from the companionship of people of all ages. And there are millions more like me. Right now, we can use your help. . . .

Such was the beginning of the Gray Panthers. They are well known by now and are a tremendous political and social force in many cities.

Helping Unexpectedly

Finally, you may find the area of need with your name on it simply by means of a serendipity. You set out to do one thing and get caught up along the way in something quite different which then becomes your special cause. For example, a high school music teacher in Illinois read in his newspaper about a man who had been in an institution for the retarded in that state for twenty-two years. Since he was brought to the institution as an abandoned baby, he had never had a visitor. The story also mentioned that he loved playing the trombone and singing but he had never had a lesson.

Deeply moved, the music teacher determined to go and teach that man to play the trombone and sing even though the hospital was a hundred and fifty miles away. However, it was apparent during the first lesson that his teaching efforts were not welcome. It seemed that the man enjoyed his own discordant sounds just the way they came out—no music teacher needed.

But the story is not over. For the music teacher realized that what was really needed was a friend. For some time now he has been traveling three hundred miles round trip once a month to visit, just to be that friend.

A similar "accidental" ministry developed in Pittsburgh a number of years ago through a group called the Pittsburgh Experiment. Some business and professional people were trying to put their Christian faith to work in downtown Pittsburgh. Because of an economic recession, one of the major problems for businessmen at that time was unemployment. This group began to organize lunches for the unemployed to help with job placement and to alert them to job opportunities. Before long, they realized that people who had been out of work a long time sometimes become emotionally unemployable. With their defeatist attitude and low self-worth, the chances are such people would blow a job interview even if they got one. Instead of centering on job placement, a group was formed to help the unemployed overcome these self-defeating attitudes. Over the years hundreds of men and women have been helped to find jobs because of the work of this group. But an Unemployables Anonymous group was not their original plan at all.

Long-range Goals

As we struggle with God's strategy for becoming helpers, I think we must always consider the long-range possibilities. In other words, we have to count the cost both for now and for the future. To begin with, we will probably need to start small, to take on one individual or a very small group. But we must be aware that if this effort succeeds, we may have a much larger mission on our hands very soon. Bea Decker, who started the one small group for widows, now leads a national movement. I'm sure Maggie Kuhn and her Gray Panthers never expected to go from one action group in a neighborhood to a national stage.

How Can Our Helping Reproduce Itself?

Next, we need to think about whether the kind of help we are offering has any chance of reproducing itself. Certainly when people are hungry we give them food, but our concern should be much broader than that. One of the great church-related movements of the last twenty-five years is World Neighbors founded by my friend John Peters. I love their slogan: "A hand up, not a hand out." They are helping economically depressed people all over the world in the name of Christ. I've heard John say many times that if a man is hungry it is not enough to give him a fish. We need to teach him how to fish. Now granted, on an emergency basis we may just give hungry people a fish. But as a long-range objective, we need to think of ways to multiply that kind of help.

For example, if we visit a lonely person in a nursing home, we're doing a kind and loving act. We may even be reminding them by our friendship that God loves them. Beyond that, whether we are thinking about nursing homes, jails, or orphanages, we need to ask, "How could I teach this lonely person to build community right here with the resources at hand?" In other words, this person will be lonely again shortly after my visit. But if I can help him or her begin to relate to others in such a way that their shared loneliness will support and encourage each other, the whole trend toward increased isolation might be reversed.

We Must Allow People to Fail

I would suggest one last long-range consideration for a helping strategy and that is that sometimes we must allow people to fail. A friend of ours, Walter Lechler, is a brilliant psychiatrist in Germany who heads up a large residential community for alcoholics and neurotics. In a discussion a few years back, he was lamenting the fact that no one is allowed to fail any more in Germany. In the old days the best families sent their "black sheep" to America. After a lifetime of failure in Europe where they were supported, subsidized, and protected by their families, they were finally given a one-way ticket to America, a frontier with no welfare programs, where they had to make it on their own. He said to me, "Your country was made great by many of those 'black sheep' who never made it at home. When failure was a possibility, they found resources in themselves to achieve many of the things that made your country a great nation."

Certainly I believe in a government that tries to insure that no citizen is homeless or cold or hungry. But while I believe this ethically and theologically, I understand, as a clinician, what my friend was saying. Where people cannot fail, they also are kept from succeeding. Sometimes in our one-to-one relationship with someone who is struggling, the best thing we can do is nothing. We can be there and we can love such persons, but any overt efforts to save them from facing themselves will only make the situation worse.

We are only free to let people fail in a situation or relationship if we believe that we are in league with God and that he has a wiser and more excellent way for each of the people we are dealing with, including ourselves. If we believe in a Holy Spirit who will guide us when our "reasonable ideas" run out, we will know more about how to help, when to help, and when not to help. And if our strategies for helping are expressions of God's love, we'll be helping in a way that honors the other person and helps him to grow through success . . . or through failure.

MEMORANDUM

TO: Keith

FROM: Bruce

RE: Chapter Six—A Place to Begin

Dear Keith,

When I read over my part of this chapter it occurred to me that it might be helpful if you'd add something about how our individual efforts to help and to bring about change are tied into God's plans. Also, I think a lot of people have strange ideas about Christianity and don't know how it might **feel** to help as a Christian.

Perhaps most of all we Christians want to know how to find God's will in terms of the right place to begin our helping efforts. Would you cover that? How **do** you determine what God's will is for you?

Haze is cooking up a storm today using the new Crockpot you gave her. I think we're going to have chicken à la Miller— or something.

Bruce

"Finding God's will." It sounds like some sort of magic—to say we can know what God's will is for us. As I read the Bible and the lives of the saints, I saw that God has always called people to particular personal or social problems or needs if and when they would seek to know his will. Could God still help people to find the particular shape of their own obedience in the last part of the twentieth century? I wondered.

Let me give you a down-to-earth illustration of how I now think we might know someone's will. Think back when you were a child. Let's say that you are walking around your neighborhood and you see a pair of roller skates in the front yard of someone you don't know. You steal the roller skates, bring them home, and hide them under your bed. Your father discovers this theft. What would his reaction be?

In my case, I know that my father would have talked to me sternly about dishonesty and stealing and told me, "We don't do that in our family." And he would have made me take the skates back, confess, and give them to the person who owned them. And I'd probably have been grounded for a few days.

Do you know what *your* father would have done? I have asked dozens of people this. And almost without exception, they've said they knew pretty well what their parent would do in this circumstance. I asked them how they could possibly know—it has been years since they were children and their father is not even with them now (mine died over twenty-five years ago). And yet they are almost all sure of what their human father's will would be. When I asked how they knew, they said that they knew his will because they had lived with him for years, they'd watched him, and listened to what he said on all kinds of subjects. And they'd watched him in relationships with other people.

I think this is something like the way we learn to know God's will in a specific situation. First we have to spend a lot of time with him and with people who are in touch with him. It's not magic, and it doesn't happen overnight. The first step for me was to try to commit my whole life to him and to the finding and doing of

113

his will for me. Then I began the kind of relationship with him and his people which would allow me to see the sorts of things his will might include for me in specific helping situations. As I read the Bible and prayed and talked to people in small groups who were also trying to find God's will, I learned more and more of the kinds of loving and effective help God has given throughout the Bible, the church's history, and in the lives of other Christians. Through confession and creative sharing with other Christians I began to know more about what the real *me* is like. And finally I am coming to have more of an assurance of what kinds of helping are God's will for *me*. And they are not at all the grim sorts of things I feared, but things which make me feel better about myself and about life—like writing and counseling with people I may meet on the journey, as God introduces me to them.

What Would Loving People the Way Christ Did Feel Like?

I remember once at a ministers' conference I was attending as a layman there was a meditation on the person of Christ. One of the ministers said, out of the silence in a kind of awe, "I wonder how it would feel to love people the way Jesus loved them?"—implying that there would be a glorious religious experience involved. A period of silence followed, and finally an older minister said, "Well, I don't think you'd ever know. Because if you were loving people the way Jesus loved them, you wouldn't be thinking about how you were feeling. You'd be totally absorbed in the other person's problem."

That comment showed me that I had some very wrong notions about what it would be like if I really gave myself to Christ and the doing of his will. And to my surprise, I realized that trying to live for God *didn't feel religious*—as I'd always thought it would. Instead of feeling more *religious,* I felt more *honest,* because I'd been forgiven and didn't have to hide so much behind religious perfection. Sometimes I was angry with God. Sometimes I loved him passionately. Sometimes I wanted to do his will, but sometimes I didn't at all. I was much more at home with myself and with most other people, but I couldn't imagine such changing feelings could be "Christian."

But now after much reading about the lives of great Christians, I think we would be amazed if we could look into the souls of some of the men and women the church has called its saints. Although they had their glorious moments, I think they felt very incomplete and uncommitted much of the time, often discouraged and lost, confused and frustrated, lustful and tired of the whole business of trying to live for God and other people on many occasions. Bonhoeffer referred to his lack of feeling certain, even while he was helping his fellow prisoners to trust in God and find comfort and strength. While the New Testament refers to Abraham's unconquerable and unswerving faith, the Old Testament shows us the dramatic ups and downs that his faith went through.

As I talk to men and women who have been deeply involved in helping others, they often tell me that they were so discouraged part of the time, so angry with the people they were trying to help because they wouldn't respond, so put out because they weren't succeeding and people were laughing at them, that they kept going partly on pride, partly on hard-headedness, and partly on faith. And yet history looks *back* on their efforts at the end of their lives and sees them to be so calm and serene. They seem to have such clear uncluttered minds. And we forget or repress the fact that in the midst of their greatest days as Christ's helpers they were only "praying and then taking educated guesses" about what God's will was much of the time. So I think most of us will wait forever if we are waiting for a glorious religious *feeling* of certainty to guide us into significant places to help. I find I must commit myself to Christ, try to determine what God's will is for *me,* and then risk moving in the direction I come up with.

God Is Already Out There Ahead of Us

Several years ago at a retreat at the Church of the Saviour, Gordon Cosby helped me realize something I'd never sensed about our beginning to "go out" to help people: since God is operating in the whole world and not just through our lives, he is *already* active in all potential helping situations, moving in people's lives *before we get there.* I know this seems simplistic, but since God has chosen to use us as the hands and feet of Christ's body in the world, I believe he is *preparing a way* for us to help in every situation. He is preparing people's hearts to be ready to turn from their lostness and pain, to turn from their sins, to look for help. We may be only a small part of a larger process in their lives. We may think we fail, but the confrontation with us may lead persons to change after we leave them. Then they may look to him so that they can begin to receive healing, hope, or even a new life.

It seems to me that we are not to "drop" help on people indiscriminately as much as we are to watch and listen and to be God's sensitive assistants in some of their changing situations. But this means we must be more acutely aware of people as well as God. The problem with some of our Christian helping programs is that we assume everyone is ready *at any and all times* for the help *our program offers.*

For instance, some evangelistic programs assume that their "life-changing encounter with God" is something everybody is ready for *at any time.* So Christians grab their materials, pray, and take off on calling programs aimed at commitment to Christ in one interview. And since everyone *does* need God, a method which calls people's attention to that need through clever questioning may have phenomenal initial success numerically. *But* the Bible emphasizes that there is a proper *time* at which God reveals himself, his help, and at which he calls on people for commitment and help. And sensitive evangelists have always advised investigating to see if the fruit is ripe before trying to tear it off the limb.

If we are only thinking about our program and not getting to know people, listening to them and to God so we can hear if this is the proper time, then we may miss getting in on some of the greatest things God is doing. And we may also inadvertently drive people away from God by our insensitivity to them and their needs.

So if God is out ahead of us preparing lives to be opened and to receive help, then part of our job is to be the midwives, the channels, of his help. If this is true, then even if we seem to do great things through our programs among people who are *not* ready for the help we have to give, we may miss our real work and those *miracles* of change *God* has ready to happen will go undone.

If we are humble and obedient and just walk down the road ahead trying to be sensitive to God and other persons, we may help them find solutions to their problems and also a new kind of wholeness. Over the years when I've tried to live this way, I have found myself miraculously at the right place at the precise time to meet someone God has ready to come to him for help. Of course this may be coincidence, but the coincidences increase remarkably when I am aware of people more than my programs.

God has promised us something of his own wisdom about his

will if we will come to him in prayer and bring with us the needs of the people in the world around us.

Some Examples of Holy Spiritual Wisdom

The way we find and use this kind of wisdom first came to my attention in a small group in an Episcopal church in Austin, Texas. We had been praying together and trying to learn how to live for God in our church and in our families and neighborhoods. Later, we were attempting to find out what we could do as a group to help the people in our city.

We decided that for one week we'd read the newspaper instead of the Bible. Every time we came across something which hurt us or disturbed us deeply, we were to cut it out and bring it to the next meeting. Different people brought different articles and news stories. But one woman named B. B. said she had never realized that there were people in Austin who were hungry. She had been reading about families in certain areas of the city not getting enough food and particularly not getting enough protein. Most of the rest of us hadn't noticed that. But we didn't know what we could do in any case, since we didn't have a lot of money or power at our disposal. I suggested to B. B. that we all pray about what we might do that week and see what we came up with.

The next week B. B. came back very excited. She said that God had given her a way that we could feed the hungry people of Austin. We all looked at her skeptically. She said her husband had a hunting ranch where people came and paid to hunt deer, wild turkeys, and other kinds of game. Most people who shoot deer put them over their car hoods and take them home to have the head mounted, and then either throw the meat away or have it frozen. Often the meat is neglected, only to be thrown out the next year and the process repeated. "Wouldn't it be great," she said, "if we could get some of these people to give their deer to us to feed the poor with?"

In the next couple of weeks, she and several other women got together and began to try to figure out how they could help this dream to happen. The system they came up with involved the following steps: They got a locker plant owner to agree to store the meat. They then got the butcher at the locker plant to process the meat— in exchange for the hides and horns, I believe. (At any rate there was very little cost to that.) They got the radio stations to put free spots on the air, telling the hunters to "give their deer to the poor." They had difficulty in finding a way to get the meat to the poor people, but eventually a Catholic group, Caritas, agreed to pick up the meat at the locker plant and distribute it to people who needed it. Then these women in our group made signs and put them in the sporting goods stores where ammunition and guns were sold and in locker plants and other places hunters go.

That year, at almost no cost at all, hundreds of people got meat who hadn't had any for a long time.

About eight years later I went back to Austin, having moved away in the meantime, and ran into the head of the Caritas organization. I asked him if they ever followed up on that "feed your deer to the poor program." "Oh, yes," he said. "We have fed tens of thousands of people meat over the years, and the program is bigger now than it ever was."

One minister I know took this idea seriously that people should minister out of problems they were drawn to. But he gave the idea a slight twist by saying he thought they should learn to minister out of *their own problems.* Making this notion the principle of his pastoral ministry, he wrote the names of members of his congregation and the tragedies they had in their lives on 3 x 5 cards he kept in his pocket. For instance, one person had been an alcoholic, another had lost a child in a car wreck, another had gone broke, another had lost his job in the middle years, another had been divorced, another had undergone a long and crippling illness, another had had a nervous breakdown and recovered. When he went calling and discovered someone in trouble, or when a counselee came to him with an agonizing situation, he reached in his pocket and pulled out the card with the name and address of the person in his congregation who had had the same problem. He asked his counselee if he or she would like to talk to someone who had been through the same difficulty and survived. Then he made contact and got these people introduced. Time after time he found that the people who had been through alcoholism, sickness, failure, or divorce were much better able to tell those who were in the midst of these experiences that they would survive and to give them some hints as to how. This also made ministers out of his congregation and allowed the pastor to be a much more effective counselor, since he was learning from his parishioners who were counseling, as well as from the counselees.

God Knows Where We'll Be Most "Efficient"

This notion of looking at the needs around us through the lens of our own intuitive inclinations and our own pain is an extremely important approach to loving. Many assume (falsely) that good ways to go about helping people sort of exist in a vacuum waiting for enough dedicated men and women to carry them out. But this is not true. Sometimes, in fact most often, the best ideas about solving a problem are not even thought of until the pressure of the problem is felt acutely by someone in the midst of it.

It is also true that an idea or solution which failed years ago might work perfectly today. When a boulder is teetering on the edge of a cliff, a child can send it careening down a mountainside and kill the dragon, when a hundred men might not have moved the same stone to the edge. If we let God lead us to the boulder, we may find one that needs just our size of shove.

As we find what we can do to help in this way, we really have a way of finding what we can do to *live* more richly. For I'm discovering that for me the way to live most fully somehow comes in helping bridge the pain-gaps in people's lives. And we bridge these gaps through the experience gained in our own pain and sin. As I find what I can do to help, I find a way of living which gives my own pain meaning and value to others, to God, and finally to myself.

Chapter Seven

Our Resources for Helping

MEMORANDUM

TO: Bruce

FROM: Keith

RE: Chapter Seven—Our Resources for Helping

Dear Bruce,

I'm a classic case of the person you mentioned last night who has felt, "What can I, an individual person without the resources of wealth or political connections, do to change things?" Why don't you start your section on resources by talking about the myth of powerlessness we discussed?

What are some of the steps we should take to discover our realistic resources? And what kinds of resources should we look for? I hope you'll give some practical examples of the use of the various kinds of resources.

Sometimes I get jealous because your examples seem better than mine. But one consolation is that the readers will get us mixed up after they put the book down—and maybe they'll think your illustrations are mine!

Keith

An English bishop once said, "Everywhere Paul went there was a revolution, while everywhere I go they serve tea." We Christians are called to "turn the world upside down," but all too often we feel like the bishop. Certainly I know how he feels. But I have always excused myself because of an awareness of my own lack of resources.

I first met Paul Tournier face to face in New York City on a cold winter afternoon many years ago. He was preaching to a capacity audience at Fifth Avenue Presbyterian Church. His opening words were electric: "Every Christian needs two conversions—the first out of the world and the second back into it."

A second conversion—back into the world. What a profound statement—earth-shaking, electric! A true believer is a revolutionary. Things should be noticeably different for at least a few people because of each person in whom Christ lives. And we wouldn't be given this charge if there weren't resources available for us to carry it out.

The Myth of Powerlessness

It is easy to say in our frustration, "But what can I do?" Possibly we feel a genuine call to help a handful of needy people, to support a worthy cause, or to start a movement. But at the same time we feel a sense of helplessness—our resources seem limited . . . and what can *one* person do? I think most of us are victims of the myth of powerlessness. Actually each of us has more resources to use for God and our fellowmen than we have ever imagined.

Near where I live in Florida there is a remarkable work going on. Dunklin Memorial camp adjacent to Lake Okeechobee provides a place for many people in trouble. There is a residential facility that can house and care for about forty alcoholics at any given time, a resource center to provide spiritual and psychological help for those with marital or emotional problems, and an expanding training center for maximum security prisoners.

This camp, which has no denominational affiliation and is supported entirely by gifts and the efforts of the camp participants,

123

was the dream of just one couple, Mickey and Laura May Evans. Its sole purpose was to provide Christian resources for people in trouble in Florida. Mickey, a Baptist minister, left the comfort of his church to start this new ministry. He and Laura May had no money and no backing and no credentials. All they had was a God-given dream.

Their first move was to sign a purchase agreement for a large tract of land on which to raise pigs and cattle to help defray the cost of overhead. And the very day they bought the land, they sold a portion of it in order to make the down payment on the whole tract. The transaction seemed miraculous—a couple with a dream and no visible backing discovered that resources were available when they were obedient to that dream.

Giving Our All

Sometimes the Holy Spirit seems to give us extra power only after we have, like Mickey and Laura May, invested everything we have in a cause or a purpose. For example, it was only after Abraham sold most of his goods, packed up the rest, and moved out in obedience to God, in spite of the risk involved, that the Holy Spirit led him to a new land and a new life. I firmly believe that as we use this model of affirmative action, we have a right to expect the extra resources of the Holy Spirit in addition to the resources we have already committed to the cause.

Taking Inventory

But having committed ourselves to a particular cause or ministry, the next step is to take an inventory of our resources. We are all too prone to cry, "Who am I? What can I do? I haven't the resources to attempt this. I am only one insignificant person." But actually, *all* of us have far more resources than we think. To overlook our resources or complain that they are limited is an insult to the goodness and greatness of God in our lives! In fact in one sense I am my resources and my resources are me—even if I am blind to the power or potential of my personality. I cannot commit my cause to God without also giving him all of me—all of my resources.

First in our inventory of resources are the obvious ones: talents, skills, time, education, money. But in addition to these, we possess vast hidden resources that are less obvious though just as powerful and just as tangible. Let's look at some of these.

Influence. Everyone has a certain circle of friends, acquaintances, colleagues, and neighbors. Whether they esteem us highly or just tolerate us, they know us and are therefore a potential resource. We have access to them. And of course, when these people have a genuine esteem and liking for us, they can be valuable resources. We can use our influence to enlist them in creative and worthy causes whether we are routinely collecting for the Red Cross on our block or organizing a cleanup campaign for some needy area.

Job and Titles. Most of us have jobs or titles, whether paid or voluntary, that give us prestige in the eyes of others. The title may mean little and the job may be menial, but to others they spell "responsibility." Often people with very menial jobs become pivotal people in a revolution. The book *The Ugly American* tells the story of twelve laboring men who met in secret with a Roman Catholic priest after the Communists took over their Asian nation. On the basis of their pooled information they had enough knowledge of the Communist apparatus to lead a grass roots revolution and overthrow the Communist government.

Health. Your health is a valuable resource. Good health is as important and in some cases even more important than time and money and talents. The cause or ministry we've committed ourselves to is going to require stamina, and stamina is one result of good health. Still, it is amazing how much people with poor health have accomplished—as in the case of Charles Darwin who, though his health was so fragile he could work only three hours a day, produced a prodigious volume of writing and research in his lifetime.

Last year Keith and I took a trip to Israel, at the hottest possible time of year in that region. We were impressed by the distances covered on foot over difficult terrain by that early handful of disciples. They traveled unceasingly in the unbearable heat of summer and the penetrating cold of that region's winter. Without the resources of health and stamina it would have been an impossible task.

But there are times when even ill health can provide a resource for working with and for others with similar health problems. In recent years, people like Betty Ford and Shirley Temple Black have been powerful models for women facing the frightening prospect of breast cancer.

Age. Whatever your age, it can be a resource. It's easy to slough off my responsibilities by pretending that my age is a deficit. When

I was young, I wished I were older and had more status and commanded more respect. Now that I am older I wish I were younger and more attuned to and negotiable with young people.

In reality, the young have influence with some and the old have influence with others. The middle-aged have an especially large amount of influence. By middle age many of us have acquired some degree of economic security, job status, affluence. And these assets can provide a resource for both the young and the elderly.

Some years ago I had a friend who was a youth minister at a large Baptist church in the Midwest. He was doing an outstanding job with young people, but in the midst of that successful ministry, God called him to work with older men—pensioners, drifters, the lonely, and the retired. My young friend took a room in the town's cheapest hotel where a number of these older men lived.

I remember so well visiting him there and having coffee with him and some of the other residents. The room was shabby and drab. Light came from one lone bulb hanging from the ceiling by its cord. Twenty-six people on his floor shared one toilet. But this sensitive young man found he could be a priest to some of the forgotten men in his town. His youth was in no sense a hindrance. His ministry there was as effective as it was to the young people of his church.

Experience. We are realizing finally that some of our best equipment for life may come not from formal education but from experience. Every success or failure, every job attempted, every heartbreak endured, every relationship, every circumstance has been fed into our computer and provides a tremendous resource for understanding life and people.

Indignation. As a rule, indignation is perceived as a negative emotion, but it can be a powerful resource. It is the emotion which prompts people to stop fights, to interrupt at meetings with shouts and protests, to circulate petitions, or even to run for political office. Righteous indignation is the emotion which prompted Jesus to take a whip and drive the money-changers from the Temple. All too often we in the church have tried to stifle this kind of indignation, to smooth it over lest we spoil our unruffled image and rock the boat. I believe we need to rediscover the gift of indignation. Outrage, one form of indignation, can be a great motivator. Outrage prompted Rosa Parks to refuse to yield her seat in the front of the bus and thereby spark a nationwide human rights struggle.

My godmother was a remarkable woman. She came from Sweden

alone and uneducated but she became a nurse, a hospital administrator, a lawyer, and a medical doctor. Later in life, just to keep her mind sharp, she earned a graduate degree in higher mathematics. But she was also a one-woman crusade and she gave much of her time to providing medical care for the poor and needy in Chicago.

Her indignation knew no bounds one day when she descended from the elevated train at Sheridan Road to find the street full of dirt and litter. Furious, she went into every shop, store, and restaurant within that two-block area and demanded to see the owner or the manager. Leading him outside, she pointed out the mess and lectured him on his responsibilities to the neighborhood. Of course, each of these people protested that the garbage pickup was irregular and, after all, what could only one person do about it? But I noticed that for some months afterward, that street was far cleaner—one woman's outrage had been contagious.

Persistence and patience. I've put persistence and patience together because they are inseparable attributes as resources. If I am to be persistent, I must have patience. And when we have creative patience, we are prepared to hang in there, to keep the pressure on, for the long haul.

A friend of mine has this resource in abundance. While still a young man, Keith Leenhouts became a judge in the misdemeanant court of his suburban community in Michigan. Most of the offenders who turned up in his court were teenagers, and he was uncertain exactly how to deal with them. Jail terms didn't appear to be a solution to their problems and certainly they are a poor means of rehabilitation.

He decided to consult a psychiatrist friend about a typical case, involving a young man who had stolen a car, drunk too much, and smashed the car. After studying the dossier on the case and interviewing the boy, the psychiatrist was not very encouraging. He said, "Judge, I'm afraid there is nothing I can do for this young man. He has what we call a character disorder. He acts on impulse without regard for the consequences."

The judge persisted, "Isn't there some existing program to help a young man like this?"

"Not really," was the answer. "And it's not an unusual situation. Eighty-five percent of these offenders will be people with character disorders. What they need is contact with other people who can provide a good example of a better way to live. Punishment alone won't change them. You have to insert inspiring personalities into their lives."

There and then Judge Leenhouts determined to do this somehow. He asked eight of his friends, including the psychiatrist, to help him establish a new program for the rehabilitation of misdemeanants with character disorders. Most of these friends had little or no psychological or theological training. Nevertheless, when these eight men began to act as sponsors for youngsters in trouble with the law and to become their friends and confidants, there were discernible results. Young people who would otherwise have been shunted into jail or released to continue the old way of life were finding positive patterns for living.

Eventually, more than five hundred people were taking part in the program, and the rate of rehabilitation in Judge Leenhouts's court more than tripled. Today, he heads up a nationwide program, harnessing the resources of lay people to help rehabilitate young people. He is tangible proof of the power of persistence and patience—and the availability of resources where none seemed to exist.

Compassion.   Compassion is a pivotal resource—it means feeling enough empathy and sympathy for others to do something about their need.

I know a manufacturer in a Texas town who was trying earnestly to find God's will for his life. One day he and a number of other businessmen from around the country were summoned to Washington by the President. They were asked to help on a local scale with a program for hardcore unemployables—people in our society who cannot get a job or keep a job for one reason or another. He prayed about his part in all this. But he didn't even know any unemployables in his town. They didn't play golf at his country club or move in his circles in any way. But he could not deny that God, through the President, was calling him to help with a major social problem of that time.

The first thing he did was to find out who these unemployable neighbors were. Compassion for their situation moved him to call on other manufacturers and managers in town to enlist their cooperation. They began a program jointly to employ thousands of people previously considered unemployable. That program was the outgrowth of my friend's compassion. And the kind of specific interest which was shown in the "unemployables" made many of them feel the sense of worth which could make them dependable workers.

The Ultimate Resource

Love. Love is certainly the ultimate resource. To me, Christian love is compassion carried even further. God so loved us that he sent Jesus to live among us and suffer with us and finally to suffer at our hands. It is love that makes us want the best even for our enemies, not just for our friends. The resource of love alone can accomplish miracles.

A few years ago in New Jersey an elderly lady was brutally beaten and murdered by a young teenager for the money in her purse—one dollar and fifty cents. Her daughter, a friend of mine, was angry and understandably bitter about this senseless crime.

But in the time since, through the help of her weekly prayer group, my friend Barbara has come to quite a different attitude. She has written to her mother's murderer in prison, forgiven him, and even visited him. She is petitioning to have him placed in her custody when he is paroled.

This kind of love does not come with degrees or experience or training. It cannot be packaged or sold. It is a gift of God. Putting this resource to work in the arena of human need can result in miracles.

MEMORANDUM

TO: Keith

FROM: Bruce

RE: Chapter Seven—Our Resources for Helping

Dear Keith,

In my section I've talked about some hidden resources we all have—some of which we've never really considered resources. But I hope you'll talk more personally about your own resources— or the ones you've been finding in recent years. Were they there all along? I'd like to hear about the resources you found to do some of the things you've done in your lifetime—like writing books, directing a lay center, counseling, or public speaking. What do you think is your most powerful resource?

It's really fun doing this book with you. But I've never felt so much resistance to writing as I've sat down and faced some of these subjects. I have the feeling God is trying to get to me with a message about changing my own life. Maybe this whole book is really for us.

Bruce

I firmly believe that the most effective resources we Christians have for use in loving and helping other people are often hidden from the world and even from ourselves. As children all of us seem to be so busy trying to earn the love of our parents and peers that we often repress, or at least keep out of sight from others, any abilities and enthusiasms which we think "they" would not approve, and therefore which would not earn us their love and their affirmation.

This "hiding" may account for the fact that some people are called to do things they are apparently not prepared for at all. And yet in some strange, deeper sense they *are* prepared, perhaps by a buried talent or perhaps by an experience of pain they have had or lived through with another—and which they have never mentioned. And such people in an atmosphere of love and commitment may find themselves responding to the call to correct a certain kind of pain or separation which no one would have suspected they had the desire or other resources to tackle. I have seen it happen dozens of times.

But how does one let God uncover his or her particular hidden resources for a task he or she feels called to do?

Beginning with Commitment

Some years ago when I first became a Christian, I was very upset because there were no models that I could see for being a Christian *and* a businessman. The few Christian businessmen I had known at a distance seemed pretty plastic and mechanical about their "witness." They carried tracts and Bibles around and offended many of the people I knew in the business world. I remember thinking that there must be a better way to witness to the kind of people I knew. The existing methods were so foreign to my own natural ways of communicating that I was tempted to assume that I was not cut out to be a witness in my business situation, except by the way I did my work.

131

I had some ideas concerning talking about the faith to business people, but this took more time than passing out tracts. And besides, if people began to believe what I was believing, it would take a lot more time to talk to them about their questions and help them reorient their lives—and I didn't have any extra time.*

But I kept seeing the loneliness and discouragement in the lives of some of the people around me. And I prayed that God would show me what to do to provide a way and a context in which business people might be able to discuss their faith intelligently and make specific commitments of their lives to God. My concern kept bugging me until finally I began to daydream about what might be effective. I imagined people coming to some sort of lay center at which they could begin to discuss their lives and the way God might relate to them and help them relate to other people. But I resisted the idea of quitting my job and working at such a project. For months I argued back and forth with God and myself. Finally I said, "All right, God, I'm tired of fighting you. If there is a way for me to do this kind of work, I'm willing to try it."

Now according to what I had believed about Christian helping, a way should have immediately opened for me to get at the work I had committed myself to do. But this was not the case. As a matter of fact, nothing happened. And so I forgot about my prayer. I went back to work at my job a little more relaxed, though, because I wasn't fighting God all day about my willingness to do his will.

Learning Where I Live

In looking back, I can see that when I made my prayer of commitment in which I said I'd be willing to work in a center for lay persons, I had neither the know-how nor the resources to do anything—even if God had dropped a lay center in my lap.

Since I didn't get an "answer," I figured I must have been mistaken about the "call." So I began doing what I could to learn about the business people around me. For several years I had been reading the Bible and praying in the mornings. But now I began to concentrate

---

* Part of the following experience was also referred to in *The Taste of New Wine* but in a different context and to a different point.

on the people around me in the office in which I worked. Not knowing what to do, I began to pray for each of them as I walked to the drinking fountain, for instance.

This decision made it necessary to get to know people personally, because I had to have something specific to pray about. So I asked questions during coffee breaks and learned about their lives—even though they didn't know I was going to use that information to pray for them more specifically. People began to come into my office and sit down to talk about their personal problems, hopes and dreams. And I hadn't even invited them to or told them what I was doing. Soon I was finding that the people around me were an amazingly needy bunch of men and women, just as I was, and that they *didn't* laugh at me or reject me when we talked about God and hope and meaning for our lives. And I began to learn how to talk to them in ways which seemed natural to me. My sense of humor, my story-telling ability (which before had been used mostly to tell risqué stories)—in fact all kinds of personal resources—were brought into this attempt to witness to business people and to help them find the shape of their own most creative obedience to God.

But the point is that God *didn't* answer my prayer about a center where business and professional people could meet to talk about their faith. Instead I began to learn how to talk to and listen to people discuss their faith *in the business world where I lived,* and to discover my own inner resources for this task. And I forgot all about my prayer of commitment to find a way to relate to people at a retreat center.

It wasn't until two years later that Howard Butt called me at 11:00 one night—his very first call to me—and asked if I would like to come down and visit their family ranch in Texas. I was living in Norman, Oklahoma, at the time. I had no idea what to say, since I really didn't know Howard except by reputation as a committed Christian businessman. As we were talking, he said that he was just finishing the building of a lay center which was going to be for the conversion and education of Christian business and professional people and their families. He'd heard me speak about my experiences in business as a Christian and thought I might be interested in his center. I told him I'd come. The minute I saw Laity Lodge I had the eeriest feeling that I would be the first director of that center. A year later, after the Lodge was finished, I did become the first director.

God Uses What You Have, Not What You Think
You Should Have

Even then I realized that I had no formal preparation nor obvious resources for being director of a conference center. I had only been to one weekend Christian conference and that was some years before. As a matter of fact, I had never liked to go to religious conferences. That's why I'd only been to one. But I had three things which constituted the preparation and resources God had given me after I'd told him I was willing to work in a center. (1) I'd been reading the Bible, praying, and trying to find God's will for me for several years. (2) I had a passionate desire to help lay people (including me) find God, and learn to live creatively, free of the fears and guilts of modern life. And (3) I had waded into the problem of working in a business office and learning how to live as a Christian myself.

The most amazing thing God showed me about my resources to run a retreat center was that he was going to use my *secular social* training instead of only my *religious* training. After two years of trying to hammer out a life as a Christian in the oil business, I was convinced that most lay people don't want to be "religious" in the pious sense, but they do want to find out about the living God and to discover a creative way to live with a strong sense of meaning and purpose. I realized that people wanted to discuss the problems and joys of living with God in their lives in the same *language* and *thought patterns* with which they discussed business, sports, children, or making love. And my natural resources were perfect for that kind of social context.

So when we started having retreats, those of us on the staff imagined that we were inviting people to our private home on the river in the hill country for a visit.* When they drove up, we met them and greeted them as if they were coming on a family weekend party with us. We dressed informally and sat around the living room talking about why we had come, what our hopes and dreams for our lives were, and began to move into the most important questions of life in a natural, easy way. There wasn't the smell of a religious campground about Laity Lodge—at least so people told me—simply be-

---

* This conference center was the dream of Mrs. Howard E. Butt and Howard E. Butt, Jr., and his wife Barbara Dan. For information concerning program write to Laity Lodge, Leakey, Texas.

cause I had never been around a religious campground long enough to know what one smelled like. And we discovered that by our having a "personal-social" psychological set rather than a "religious program" psychological set, people were more ready to talk about personal things and eventually to make personal commitments to the living God.

And I was amazed to learn that the most helpful resources I brought to the conferences were the seemingly "nonreligious" experiences of trying and failing and trying again to live for Christ in the business world and trying to help other people find the shape of their lives as Christians.

Unfortunately, in the past many Christians who got turned on about helping in God's kingdom were told that such interest and commitment are signs of a call to go to theological seminary to become ordained ministers—which may or may not be true. But when this happens, people are often sent to seminary *without letting God work on them and teach them their particular vocation and resources in the context in which they heard his call.* One may discover in this period of "living with the questions," the specific nature of the ministry he or she is called to and some creative and unique resources and ideas which he might never find in a theological school.

Helping People to Find and Develop Their Resources

At Laity Lodge we began to use the approach of helping people find the creative shapes of their own obedience and love and to examine their "natural" resources. We asked people what they would like to do if earning money were not a problem. I remember one woman saying she had always wanted to write. So she was helped to write one book and then another. This happened with several men and women there who had repressed lifelong desires to write. Others decided to study counseling; some got involved with special education. They were helped to find schools and scholarship aid. It was very exciting. And the kinds of helping these people subsequently did was filled with energy and enthusiasm and seemed to ignite creativity and life in those being helped, because the resources being used were natural and charged with passion and energy. The helpers felt as if they were carriers of the gifts of the Holy Spirit rather than people dutifully putting helpful Band-aids on society's sores.

The Dormant Power Is in the People

The fact that so many people have found through this process ways in which they can use hitherto hidden abilities to help people has led Bruce and me to believe that it may be the key to the greatest hidden resource in the church—the repressed creativity and ability in the lives of its own people. When men and women begin to see the power and creativity being released in the lives of Christians with whom they can identify, they begin to dream big dreams—and implement them.

A group of men and women in Texas built Kaleo Lodge, similar to Laity Lodge, near Dallas. Creath Davis and those who committed themselves to this ministry have helped literally thousands of people over the last ten years find new life and ministries of their own to help other people.

Another man in Corpus Christi has a ministry of distributing tapes and books through a nonprofit bookstore and distribution center. Other people have bought a house where young people are helped to come off drugs and find a new life. And several others mentioned earlier have become writers and artists trying to express truths which they had never had the courage to try to release. Eulalia, a dear friend, who is the marvelous cook at Laity Lodge and who has added so much by her gifts for creative cookery, discovered on one of the creative weekends there that she had a talent for oil painting. And now she has become a professional artist, although she is still in charge of the food program at Laity Lodge. One suburban housewife began to visit prisoners in the local jail; another began to start groups at a federal penitentiary by going with them on the adventure many of you reading this book have been on with *The Edge of Adventure.* And dozens of people have started strugglers' groups in their offices or their homes or their neighborhoods in which people can begin to come to grips with their own separation and lostness and the call of Christ to become carriers of his Spirit to others. They are finding and helping others to discover the healing and creative potential God can uncover when we begin to present ourselves to him and to each other and listen to cries in the world and in our own lives to which our hearts resonate.

A Church of Unwrappers

As Bruce has pointed out so powerfully in *Ask Me to Dance,* when Jesus stood at the tomb of Lazarus and called his name, he walked out of the grave alive. This was miraculous. But all Lazarus could say, with gritted teeth, was "hallelujah." He was alive but he was totally bound in graveclothes. And the surprising thing is that Jesus never got Lazarus out of the graveclothes, according to the Scriptures. What Jesus did, instead, was turn to the people standing around Lazarus and say, "*You* unwrap him."

I think this is where many of us in the church are. We have been brought to life by Jesus Christ, but we are wrapped in the graveclothes of other people's expectations of us, sometimes from childhood. We have been wrapped in the graveclothes of our fears of disappointing other people. We have been afraid that our own hopes and dreams and inner resources would not be worthy to win the love we must have. I believe that one of the greatest ways we have to uncover hidden resources is to be in a group we have given permission to unwrap us. Then we can come out and use the hands and feet and the gifts God has given us. Many of these gifts may have become bound inside us for years by our own brokenness and lostness and that of the people around us. For all of us have somewhere hidden inside us something of the creative life Christ has promised us to use in loving the world.*

But one of the strange things I have discovered is that I *resist* being unwrapped and freed to be what I can become for Christ. I resist because I am afraid to fail. And besides, if I have a secret dream of doing something like painting or going back to school or starting a center, I can always use that *dream* as an escape from facing reality. I can always say to myself that if things go bad with what I'm doing I'll be an artist or a conference director. But if I let you unwrap me and I *try* to *fulfill* my dream in the real world, I no longer have an escape hatch if I fail. And then I will have to face reality with only God and his people as my strength and support.

The Greatest Resource

In the last three or four years I have been gradually realizing that the greatest resource I have comes to me through a particular combination of people and circumstances. This resource is the Holy

---

* If you are interested in being in a group of unwrappers trying to find their own resources and gifts to use in loving the world, Bruce and Keith have prepared a thirteen-weeks course which they lead—using this book as one of its resources. The course is called *The Passionate People,* Carriers of the Spirit. Leader's kit and manuals may be purchased from Christian bookstores or from Word, Inc., P.O. Box 1790, Waco, Texas 76703.

Spirit himself as he operates in and through the intimate community of people I've been talking about as we try to commit our lives to Christ and to learn his will for us particularly. As I have confessed my own sins and pride and fears, I find that I can accept his forgiveness. Then the past is wiped clean, and I can start writing new chapters in my life with fresh pieces of chalk.

These experiences of forgiveness and new starts take a lot of the cobwebs out of my thinking as I try to allow the Holy Spirit to give me his perspective on the problems "out there," through the help of Christian friends. And in this process I begin to see my own untried resources and abilities. But the process takes time and patience, since some of these gifts and resources have been deeply buried beneath the fears and insecurities of a lifetime.

If we really took seriously the business about having God as the primary resource in the helping situation, then we would be convinced of the underlying power we could bring with us into even the most seemingly secular problem. Because there is a kind of assurance we Christians can have, because of our experience with God and with other people—that there *really is* hope, that God actually builds the most glorious parts of his kingdom out of the broken pieces of our lives—if and when we bring them to him. And as Bruce has said, nothing is wasted—no pain, no loss, no separation. For God gives his people insight for future understanding and hope out of the pain and even the failure of the present. He forgives us and cleans the slate so that we can even eventually walk through periods of tragedy and guilt with a different kind of wisdom and understanding. And as we walk, stumble, fall and get up again, God teaches us to be carriers of this love and hope through a committed relationship to Jesus Christ and to his people. And if we are filled with the Spirit of Christ then what we are bringing at those times when we have nothing to bring except "just ourselves" is the healing renewing presence of the Living God himself.

Chapter Eight

Some Strategies for Helping and Leading

MEMORANDUM

TO: Bruce

FROM: Keith

RE: Chapter Eight—Some Strategies for Helping and Leading

Dear Bruce,

Jesus' kind of leadership seems to be so contradictory to the current corporate and institutional models that the problem of how to lead or choose leaders for a Christian helping venture has really gotten cloudy.

How about starting from small to large by talking about one-person helping campaigns? Then you've told me some neat examples of people getting together in a nonorganized way to work for social change. But I guess the thing that would be most helpful would be for you to take us through some of the process of organizing a group for action in helping others—just some step-by-step guidelines, including the question of deciding what the primary goal of your group's venture is, and who should lead. And finally, any suggestions on how the leader might help the group to function more closely together as Christians.

Keith

A few days ago I received an unsigned handwritten letter from San Francisco. The letter said, "Reverend Bruce Larson: In Christ's name, I ask you to join in the enclosed prayer and to enlist the prayer support of other Christians, especially missionaries, in this effort, that revival may come in San Francisco."

It went on to suggest that revival was not coming because of Satan's hold on a certain well-known church in San Francisco. Accompanying the letter was a two-page mimeographed indictment of that church. I was asked to pray and to send this letter on to friends.

The last paragraph said, "*God* knows who is writing this—and that's what matters! I don't want credit for this prayer drive and am not signing this. God will answer our prayers and to Him be the glory."

The One-Person Campaign

Obviously, the person who wrote this letter was not waiting to organize anything in order to bring about change. He (she) became "the leader" by simply sitting down and beginning to write letters, I suppose, to people all over the country. Organizing for change through a one-person movement is one way to go, though this particular letter prompted no action from me. (I am always suspicious of people who are focusing on some group "out there" as the cause of evil and the hindrance to their own righteousness.) But the letter arrived just as I was writing this chapter and it reminded me that similar "one-person campaigns" have occasionally resulted in large-scale changes.

For example, a century or so ago surgeons were losing a large percentage of their patients after surgery. No one seemed to know why. We can imagine a conscientious doctor of that time trying every possible means to sharpen his skills and extend his knowledge in an effort to improve those statistics.

Then, along came a doctor with a theory about something called germs. He suggested that if surgeons would simply wash their hands

141

before surgery, more patients would survive. Not only was the idea not readily accepted, but this visionary doctor was subjected to so much ridicule and humiliation that he eventually died a broken man in a mental hospital. It was not until many years later that the germ theory was recognized. Doctors began to wash their hands and the operating room death rate declined drastically.

Sometimes a one-person campaign is a tough way to promote even a brilliant and life-saving idea. But such an effort has a number of advantages. You don't have to recruit a lot of people, supervise them and delegate responsibilities. You simply begin.

Many years ago on a trip to England I met a delightful little woman at a lay renewal conference who had undertaken such a one-person campaign. Friends told me an incredible story about this frail, delicate looking woman. The child of missionaries, she was the first white woman born in Kenya, where she lived for many years. In middle age she returned to Dublin with her sister. One night during a prayer meeting, she was earnestly seeking God's will for her life. She seemed to feel that he was telling her to care for the homeless children who roamed the streets of Dublin.

Clara got up off her knees, corralled a teammate, and the two of them set off at once to patrol the city streets. That very first night they came upon a drunk who wanted to begin a new life and prayed with him. They gave shelter to a young wife who had left her husband. A work in Dublin was begun which subsequently led to the rehabilitation of hundreds of criminals, orphans, strays and drunks. God gave this brave woman her marching orders, and she immediately became involved and vulnerable. She did not set out to become a leader but to do a job. God made her a leader as she obeyed his call.

Nonorganized Social Action

While any number of organizations have grown out of the compassionate action of one person, sometimes even group action can best be carried on unofficially and without organization.

This kind of social action which lacks any official organization has many advantages. Working quietly, you often catch people without their negative defenses up and where they are vulnerable. By such quiet and unorganized methods, one person can have far-reaching effects on all of society. The key here for Christians is to use influence without slipping over the line into blackmail or unethical coercion.

A Classic Example

John Woolman, a devout Quaker, lived in the eighteenth century at the time when many wealthy Quakers were slave holders. As a young man, he vowed to rid the Society of Friends of this terrible blight, and for thirty years he gave his life to that task—unofficially.

Now, John Woolman's strategy was basic and unique. He did not picket or hold mass rallies. He didn't publish vindictive sermons against slavery and those who practiced it. Rather, over those thirty years he traveled up and down the length of the land visiting with Quaker slaveholders. He would simply accept their hospitality and ask them questions about how it felt as a child of God and as a Christian to own slaves. There was no condemnation in his approach. He believed these slaveholders were responsible people of conscience, and he asked them disturbing questions: "What does the owning of slaves do to you as a moral person?" "What kind of value system are you passing on to your children?"

His one-man campaign was so effective that one hundred years before the Civil War not a single Quaker held slaves. This was the result of one man's unorganized and unofficial social action.

Establishing a Base

Having said all of this, however, I find there are still times and circumstances when the most effective course is some kind of organized group action. What are the best ways of becoming organized? Perhaps first of all, we should look at Jesus' methods for accomplishing God's will in the world as it is demonstrated in the Gospels. Jesus' strategy was aimed at corporate groups of people, nations, and, by implication, the entire world—through individuals gathered together in his kingdom.

First, we find that Jesus began his ministry at the grass roots rather than at the top. He lived with, worked with, and taught the common people. He called them to purity and repentance and reform. So often we take the opposite approach and try to restructure from the top without providing an example or model at the grass roots which demonstrates our ultimate aims. I think, without question, that in our own attempt to organize for change, it is probably best to establish a base with some of the people around us before we tackle the power structures.

Second, Jesus set out to change the world by concentrating on a small group. This group of twelve became the primary focus of his ministry. He lavished most of his time on them. I don't mean to minimize mass communication. It is especially important today and Christians ought to be making the best possible use of the mass media. But history demonstrates that a small team of people obedient to Christ and committed to one another in love and fellowship is likely to be much more effective than a highly publicized and structured campaign.

Challenging "Authority"

Third, Jesus aimed at the very center of the power structures of his time. Ultimately he went right to Jerusalem and into the Temple, the seat of authority. The bulk of his time was not spent there, but if he was to change the religious structure of his time, the Temple at Jerusalem was a crucial target. Here is an important lesson for us; we Christians cannot confine our efforts to the grass roots. Sooner or later we must confront the centers of authority if we are to be a force in shaping society.

Next, Jesus challenged the accepted lies, myths, and half-truths of his time. Without the help of tracts or books, he took issue with the religious leaders publicly. Of course, these are the actions which led to his eventual betrayal and death. But if we are attempting a ministry which will make lasting changes in the world, we must be prepared to risk our lives and reputations as well. At some point, it is essential to "go public" with our convictions whatever the cost.

Personal Cost

Jesus' ultimate strategy involved self-sacrifice. He must have known that to continue his teaching would mean death, but he did not retreat to some safe place. Rather he sacrificed himself, and through this sacrifice the Kingdom was established. In that last night in the garden, Jesus told the soldiers who came to arrest him, "I am he—the man you are seeking." Then he pointed to the twelve disciples and said, "Let these men go" (John 18:8). All serious reformers need to understand this particular part of Jesus' strategy. It is *our* lives and *our* fortunes we offer to God, not the lives and fortunes of others.

Who Should Lead?

With all this in mind, let's consider now how one can best effectively organize for change, if an organization is necessary to accomplish the purpose God has given us. Whenever we organize, it is a fact of life that *someone* will be in charge, though that person may not necessarily hold the top title. No group, even a small and informal one, can function without some kind of an acknowledged center of authority. Any organized group requires a president, chairman, or leader. The question is, who should lead?

I remember some years ago meeting in a hotel room in mid-Manhattan with four close friends. We were dreaming about what God's next step might be for our lives together, since we felt called to a common mission and ministry. We were all deeply interested in Christian education, and in the course of the conversation, we began to dream up a new kind of school for the training of laymen and clergy. We were all excited about the possibility when someone raised the question, "But who will be president of this new school?"

There was an embarrassed silence, or I should say I felt embarrassed by the question. But actually it was a wise and pertinent question and the friend who raised it knew that unless we could resolve the flow of authority, the project would be doomed to failure before it got started.

After some discussion we were all a little startled when one man said flatly, "I want to be the president. If I can't be the president, count me out." When he went on to explain that he felt he functioned best in that kind of role, the rest of us saw immediately that he was right and agreed, relieved that our problem was solved. That school has still not passed the theory stage, but if we should ever decide to go ahead, we have crossed the first great administrative hurdle. And the person most qualified emotionally to be in charge emerged very naturally.

Who Should Not Lead?

But it's not always that easy. Sometimes there are people who aspire to the role of top leader who do not have the skills or the gifts to fulfill that role. They have the need to be in charge but do not possess the required talents. Either they don't work well with people, or they fail to make good use of the resources at hand. Unfortunately, the person who aspires to lead is not always the right choice.

Michael Korda, author of the best-seller *Power,* warns against many of the types who gravitate to power. According to Korda, we should be wary of the people who must be in control of all situations at all times. In a taxicab, they are not content with giving the driver the destination, they insist on explaining the exact route to follow to get there. That's a danger signal. This kind of a person may well have difficulty delegating authority.

Another dangerous type, according to Korda, is the person who has never come to grips with his or her own unconscious desire to have power in an organization. He likes to consider himself a humble and selfless servant when in fact he has an insatiable need for power. Unless he is in charge, making decisions, he is uncomfortable and becomes a trouble-maker. Frequently, however, when these people do accede to power they exert such a servant image outwardly that their behavior confuses those trying to follow them. They are in fact very poor leaders.

Then there is the person who consciously or unconsciously acquires power by becoming involved in the lives of all of the people around him or her who are in power. This type is unnaturally interested in other people's problems because this gives him an opportunity to be needed and to exert influence. Be careful of the person in your organization to whom everybody owes a favor while he owes no one.*

The Luxury of Group Decision

In deciding who should be in charge it is good to evaluate the urgency of the task you wish to accomplish. What is the timetable? If you have plenty of time, you can afford the luxury of a low-profile leader, one who will allow for maximum participation, input, and decision-making from all members of the organization. But if

---

* I am aware that a Christian also seems "unnaturally" interested in other people's problems. But the Christian will also probably be vulnerable about his own problems and be willing to let people help him—otherwise people will be suspicious of him too.

you are on a tight time schedule or face an emergency which may threaten your corporate existence, you need a strong leader who can bypass the supportive kind of thing and help the group to make quick decisions and act on them. There just isn't time to let everybody have maximum input. There may be laws to write, bills to defeat, elections to be held, food to be distributed, or housing to be planned, and in an emergency these things simply cannot wait until everyone has his or her say.

A Mutual Goal

A third consideration in organizing your group for action is the primary goal of the group. Only after deciding on mutual goals can you employ a strategy for accomplishing them. Let's examine a typical church committee, perhaps a building committee. I suppose that building committees have fostered more dissension and bad feelings than any other single group in the church. When a committee for the new church building meets for the first time, each member may have a picture in mind of the kind of building which will be both practical and aesthetically appealing. As the weeks go by and the architects present drawings, it seems impossible that any agreement will be reached among the devotees of the gothic structure, the fans of colonial architecture, the group who want contemporary design, and those holding out for a functional building.

A friend was the chairman of a new building committee several years ago. Before a single plan was requested from the architects, this chairman asked the committee to decide what they wanted this new building to express to people walking in for the first time. With this in mind, the committee began to rethink the whole mission of the church. When they were able to agree on the unique mission of that church in that particular place, and at that time, they were unanimous about what they wanted to convey through the building. The selection of the architectural design followed easily. Rather than presiding over the usual building committee squabbles, this chairman enabled a deeply meaningful experience for all of the committee members, and I can vouch for the uniqueness and beauty of the finished building.

And many times if any helping group asks, before beginning its work, what the members hope will happen in the lives of the people to be helped, there will be a much more natural unity and sense of agreement among the helpers.

The People versus the Official Agenda

Finally, even after you have found the best possible president or leader, never take the members of your organization for granted. Those people still require maintenance. Every organization has two agendas taking place at each meeting. There is the official agenda of the business to be conducted by the group. But each person sitting around that table has a personal agenda as well. At any given time, each member brings recent hurts or hopes, joys or pains, disappointments or resentments. Motions for consideration are affected by those emotions. Beyond that, personal hostility between committee members can affect the business agenda. Hostile reactions to a motion can sometimes be the result of hostile feelings toward the person making the motion, with no regard for the merits of the motion itself.

In my experience, if the committee or group is a Christian organization, it is best to allow ample time at the beginning of a meeting for each person to share a little of his or her personal agenda. Hold a short report time in order to hear the particular pain or joy that people bring to a meeting. And begin by sharing something real from your own life. When everyone has reported where he or she is, you might pray for one another and the situations mentioned. When Christians have been heard, loved and prayed for sincerely by God's people, the business at hand can usually be handled with far more dispatch and unity. Usually, when there is not enough time for the personal agenda, there is not enough time to finish the business agenda. This process which seems to many church leaders a "waste of time," is actually the greatest time-saver I have found, as a minister and group leader.

An Irresistible Challenge

One final word about organizing your group for action. I firmly believe that you will be much more successful if membership is demanding. Most of us want to belong to an organization because we believe in the purpose of that group and because we feel that God has called us to do something important through and with them. Without that high purpose and without the demand for high commitment, your group is doomed to failure before it gets started.

The Italian patriot Garibaldi understood this. In recruiting his army, he gave them an unusual challenge, one which evoked an overwhelming response in loyalty and numbers. Standing in the public square, Garibaldi called for recruits in this way: "Soldiers, what I have to offer you is fatigue, danger, struggle, and death; the chill of the cold night and the free air, and heat under the burning sun; no lodgings, no munitions, no provisions, but forced marches, dangerous watchposts, and continual struggle with bayonets against batteries. Those who love freedom and their country may follow me." This call to commitment got impressive results.

Jesus' call then and now is even more demanding. "Take up your cross and follow me." Now, as then, when people hear and understand his call, they follow him gladly.

MEMORANDUM

TO: Keith

FROM: Bruce

RE: Chapter Eight—Some Strategies for Helping and Leading

Dear Keith,

As I looked over my part of the last chapter, I wish I had said more about the strategies for helping we Christians are presently using which are largely ineffective. Can you tackle this and perhaps sketch in **why** they are mostly ineffective?

I used your phrase earlier—"cannon fodder for someone else's war." How do we in the church avoid feeling that we are often in this category?

We got back from Vermont last week. I think Haze is finally cured of longing for the beautiful snow country. We pushed the car out of snowdrifts each morning in ten-below temperatures. The last day I added injury to insult and broke my leg!

Bruce

Barriers to Successful Organizing

My big brother used to con me into helping him with any jobs our parents assigned him or with projects he wanted to take on. When I finally realized that he was using me instead of wanting me to be with him, my feelings were hurt, and I didn't like to help him any more.

I was thinking about that recently in terms of the way we Christians often organize for helping ventures in the church. So often the church doesn't call on us unless it needs us to help fulfill someone else's program. And I resent the way this is sometimes handled by our leaders. It may be that a guest speaker or evangelist has been invited to our church and we are needed as audience since "we don't want to disappoint him." It may be that the minister or someone on the church board has decided that we need to get more involved with the problem of dope among young people or racial discrimination in real estate, or forming a day-care center at the church so that young mothers who need to work can bring their children to be loved and taught. Or some influential member may feel that we need to get involved in the political situation in our town with regard to the inhuman treatment of prisoners, etc. And all of these may be very good causes.

Cannon Fodder for Someone Else's War

But the first thing I usually hear about such projects is when a meeting is eventually called and I am contacted to help. Often within ten minutes of the time I walk in the room I know that two or three "leaders" have met somewhere and pretty well decided what we are going to do, though the chairperson says they are looking for input from us. And I get that same conned, used feeling I felt with my brother. The passionate discovery of the cause we are asked to participate in took place somewhere else and is not shared with us. What the committee is really looking for—I suspect—is bodies, menial laborers to carry out their project. And although I realize

151

this reveals my own discovery of *my* manipulative tendencies, I still feel disinclined to help.

As I sit down in the back of the room, I realize intellectually that they will, of course, need helping hands to do this worthy work they have in mind, and I may help out of a sense of duty. But something inside me rebels at being used in an impersonal way to fulfill their project quota needs. I know this is sin and intense selfishness on my part, but somehow I get the feeling that they don't need *me,* but someone sitting in my chair—and that *anyone* would do. I just don't feel like helping when I'm treated like a labor force for their dream. I know this is not the "right way to feel" and I feel terrible about it. But as I talk to people who sit in the churches I have come to believe that many people feel this way, and that can be a very depersonalizing thing.

Business managers know that above a certain level of education and creativity, people will only support projects at a deep emotional level in which they may have some part at a planning stage. And our Lord certainly seems to have recognized this when he left the twelve to organize his church in the first century.

If you reading this are a leader in the church, you may be saying, "Keith, you don't understand. If we leaders don't do the organizing and get the program ready, the people will not support it. They simply won't take the time to do this sort of work unless we come up with a plan and organize it down to simple tasks they can handle without much effort. And there isn't time to hold the hands of the people at the meetings by hearing about their personal lives."

I know. I know. But I do not believe you. Of course if you are thinking of the church as a kind of a glorified service club, then perhaps you are right. And the way many churches operate, you would have far greater support by using your "organized" method than the "organic" one I am going to suggest. But I believe the impersonal system of getting people to help which I have just roughly described has not proved notable with regard to its positive results.

Creating an "Organic" Participating Community

How would one person (an adult male Christian, for example) take the leadership in forming an organic community from which creative helping efforts might eventually go forth into the world? There are many stages at which he could begin, but let's say he is starting from scratch, having just made a renewing commitment of his own life to Christ. And he's setting out to find God's will for him in this new chapter of his life.

If he's alone when he has the renewing experience, the person hoping to create a participating community might try to pray for one other person in his own church with whom he might share his experience of God and his longing that the church should be known above everything else as a center for loving the Lord and helping in healing the pain and lostness in the world.* After finding that one person, the man with a dream can tell him unhurriedly and privately what Christ means to him. The dream might be of a reborn church—what it might be like. He might talk about how he can see God transforming the atmosphere in a whole community through a committed team and hear the other person's questions and dreams. And if this person doesn't hear, let him find another one. Let him pray and witness until at least one other person shares his passionate hope and shares it enough to find a third member of the church while the first partner goes to a fourth. Or maybe they go together to find two more.

This process may take months. But when four are ready to go on an adventure of trying to find and do God's will in their lives, an organic type group can be born. And it begins at depth. The power of this kind of group depends on people being willing to love each other, to give themselves away to one another and to share their lives and prayers in order to join in this adventure with Christ. They are committed to learning how to live and use the creative things they have been given to live and work with. The group members become apprentices to Christ and each other.

The Leader as a Member of the Group

This certainly seems to be the New Testament way. Jesus' method (and Paul's) was that of apprenticeship. That seems almost always to be God's method of creating community. Look at Moses and Joshua, Elijah and Elisha, Jesus and the Twelve, Paul and Silas and Barnabas and Mark and their little groups. This may sound terribly naive to a sophisticated and highly organized minister of a

---

* This is certainly not a new idea. And it applies to ordained ministers as well as to lay leaders. But it is one which has been dismissed by and large as being too time-consuming. I'm assuming people who've tried alternatives might be open to trying it.

large, busy church. But history indicates that there is no shortcut to taking the time to be on a personal adventure with Christ and a few other committed people, if a genuine healing community is to be born.

The thing that sets the organic Christian group apart from other organized groups is that the minister is also an apprentice. Since nothing in the average seminary teaches ministers how to live in the secular world and find God's will for *their own lives* outside the sanctuary, this may be a threatening experience for both minister and lay people.

I think we have the idea that the seminaries are mass-producing some kind of leader-helper person who is an expert in *living* the Christian life. But it is not necessarily true that one is trained to be a *"spiritual liver"* (or leader) in seminary—even though he may be a great preacher, liturgist, and organizer. And what I am suggesting is that the training we do get in seminary comes alive and becomes really usable when we professionals go on an adventure ourselves with some of our people. We begin to understand what we have learned as we try to find out how to get *ourselves* unlocked and freed enough to love the world and to help in overcoming its pain and lostness. I think *we* as leaders have got to confess the fact that we don't know how to love people either, that we want to learn how to be the hands and feet of the Spirit of God in the world. And if anyone wants to come with us, we are willing to teach him or her all we know about God and life—as we are learning more.

Don't Promote a Product You've Never Tried

I often advise ministers and lay leaders never to promote a group unless they have been in that same kind of group, enjoyed it, and gotten something out of it themselves. (Or unless they are willing to enter the first group which starts.) In other words, if somebody comes out of seminary and promotes prayer groups in his or her parish, never having been in a group, it would be sort of like a coach telling a bunch of young people to go jump in the pool for a swim when he was a nonswimmer himself, and had never been in a pool. It is not only unwise, but dangerous.

The minister must see *himself* as needing the group in order to learn about God's will for *his own life* and the finding of his own creative resources, or the group will be hamstrung. He must want very much to learn how to live his own life for Christ. And what he is sharing is largely what he is learning on the adventure. Since the process, the living of the life for Christ, is the end, there is no pressure for "success" for the group (or the minister) in terms of the group's number or even accomplishments.

But some ministers have said, "Well, I don't want to influence the group too much, so I won't go to the meetings," or, "I'll go but I won't participate." Some have even sat in the corner of small group meetings as an "observer," refusing to say anything—which is surely the fastest way that has yet been discovered to kill openness in a group. And many *never see* the arrogant superiority their silence and nonvulnerability can communicate.

In fact, unless a leader wants to try to be as vulnerable as the people, in terms of sharing himself and his struggles, there is no way I know that he or she can lead them to be a vulnerable and caring community in which it is *really* acceptable to confess failure and receive forgiveness and new starts. Where such groups have been formed without the minister's personal participation, the true spiritual leadership has been assumed by someone else—who may not seem to be a leader at all on the parish organization chart. I am *not* saying that all churches are *supposed* to have an open vulnerable fellowship. But I am saying that if one is desired, a leader will be one who is among the chief of the vulnerable.

Leaders and Tasks Emerge Together

And the leaders which emerge in helping, praying groups will often not be persons the world has called leaders heretofore. They will be people who have committed themselves to Christ and his adventure and then found hope, courage, and untapped resources in their own lives. (E.g., look at the helpless alcoholics who have become towers of strength in AA.) Then, because of the burning motivation to do something, such leaders emerge with leadership qualities they would not have believed they had.

How does this happen? And how does the group member feel included in the creative formation of a helping venture? Let's say that your group has progressed to the place where you begin to read the newspaper occasionally as well as the Bible to find out what hurts you about the agony in your community. Or someone finds that he has a lot of pain in his life because of what's happening to some people around him who are being dispossessed or treated unfairly or who are lost and struggling for some kind of hope and meaning. Let's say that this problem becomes a part of his prayer life and he brings to the group a description of the problem and shares his own anguish over it.

After the group members have heard and questioned him, they may ask him if he sees any way to solve the problem or meet the need involved. As he talks about this, they may give him some suggestions or get more involved themselves. Other people may be led to join him in claiming the problem.

It seems to me that one of the greatest misunderstandings of Christian help is the idea that the group should "vote" on what they are going to get involved in, as if they were all supposed to do all the *same* things. People are called to different needs. This means that the man or woman who has an idea for helping people and who feels passionately about it may be able to draw three or four people from the group to go with him on his adventure for God.* And when these potential helpers decide to be a part of the helping after hearing about (and feeling in some sense) the pain of the people they are going to try to love and help, they aren't as likely to feel conned or manipulated.

But historically, *the person with the passion is the initial leader!* If someone else gets involved who is just as passionate about the problem and who has more leadership ability, the leadership may change. But usually the person who is in anguish about the problem makes the best initiating leader, because his passion can motivate others. And because he cares so deeply he will stick with the helping and be motivated to go beyond a successful beginning until something substantial can get done about the dream he has been given.

Members Choose the Adventure, the Task, and the Group

Several years ago, before Bruce and I knew each other, we each became very involved in trying to get people in the church to consider new approaches to education and small groups. Then we met and became friends. Soon we realized that God was calling us to try to live the Christian life with some kind of integrity and to share the adventure with lay men and women who might want to commit their lives and come along. When each of us found the other was on the same adventure, we decided independently to join forces.

---

* See Elizabeth O'Connor's *Journey Inward, Journey Outward* for a description of a community grappling with those issues.

That choosing seems to me to be the key. If you feel you would like to get on the adventure of helping in a certain way, then your desire to do it that way is one of the main criteria for going. And you will not feel manipulated. But if God does not give you enthusiasm for the project, then in the long run you may only be doing more harm than good by joining the group.

I guess Bruce and I are sort of using the Tom Sawyer approach to helping. We decided that we were going "to paint the fence" together whether anyone else did or not. When people came along and asked us if they could paint, we said we would let them help us if they wanted to. But we were going to paint anyway, even if they didn't. With this approach you don't wind up begging people to join you and getting them on the team just to further your project—only to find out that because they have felt conned they will be the sour apples that will ruin the whole barrel later, when things get tough.

Why Laying a Worthy Cause on People Doesn't Work

But if you happen to be a minister, you may be screaming, "Wait, Keith, you can't always meet and choose how you want to help! What if the national church sends us a notice that we are supposed to raise money to help in a particular social or educational mission? Do we have to wait until somebody in our parish feels called to lead such a campaign in our church?" In most cases I think the answer is yes.

Trying to get people to do things out of guilt has been devastating for the church. The money or personal support is almost never adequately raised in the first place. And every struggle of trying to browbeat people to help out of guilt affects the success and enthusiasm of the next project suggested. It is worth the time it takes to have the people pray and question their way into a substantial project in order to find out if that cause is God's will for them. Every cause of a jurisdictional body is not necessarily a valid cause for *every* person in the church. Of course we do commit to do many things as a family that we didn't think of ourselves. I'm only saying that a much more biblical and Christian approach would seem to be to call the group together, describe the problem, pray about it, and see if the group feels called by God to respond. Of course, in emergency or desperate short-term disasters, the community of believers will just naturally want to respond—if it is Christian.

But when a long-term helping project is being considered, participation had better be the result of a free choice process for the church and its people to see if anyone really feels called *to* this project. And if no one does, although an announcement may be required as well as putting something about the project in the bulletin, I think it is a disservice to one's people to take leadership in a demanding program one doesn't really believe in. Somehow, in the long run, the integrity of the leader and his own enthusiasm become some of the main ingredients for success in any *Christian* helping effort. For if we have not examined these questions concerning God's will for our lives, but have only done things people have told us we should do in a disinterested way, it's no wonder no one in the church wants to expend costly energy to help us with such programs.

The Challenge of the Long-term Task

Jesus spent about thirty years getting ready for his three-year ministry. And after Paul was converted, he seems to have spent three years in the desert and eight years in Tarsus before he found his place of leadership in the church. I think so many of us have a picture of leading in helping situations as if we were going to be chairman of a committee that was going to last a week or a month. Whereas it seems to me God is calling us to be a passionate people who are looking for places to learn and to help others along the way—as a way of *living our whole lives*. We are looking for a problem or a place to work and live which is our "place" and our spiritual vocation (e.g., a person might decide to be a lay church history teacher for the rest of his life, or a visitor of prisoners). We are looking for a way in which we can grow and fulfill our own lives and God's will for us and for other people.* The short-term, "instant-food" approach the church often seems to take with regard to helping appears to me to be shallow and short-sighted.

I know of no "rules" as to how the Spirit will call the Passionate People to love the world. He calls us to specific needs in specific places—so each group's life will develop in its own way. And he must wait until his people are ready to adventure with him.

---

* I realize that this may sound like some sort of pious and grim process and that committed Christians don't have fun or enjoy life. The Christians I know on this adventure are the happiest people I've ever met—in spite of the hard things they've faced.

As I read the Bible and the church's history, it becomes more and more apparent to me that God shows us people's needs in the drama of life around us. He calls his children to do loving, healing work that, humanly speaking, we would never have picked. The church would never have chosen leaders like Paul (a killer of Christians), Mary Magdalene (a loose woman), Augustine (a licentious "English" teacher), Luther (a compulsive and constipated monk), Ignatius Loyola (a wounded soldier), George Fox (an emotionally disturbed person), or people like you and me. But for each of us there are tasks that only we can do—large or small—which God has picked out for us. The miracle seems to be that God doesn't choose perfected experts but that he builds his kingdom and his leadership out of the broken pieces of our lives, if we will commit them totally to Jesus Christ, to each other, and to the problems of the world.

Chapter Nine

Your Church as Change Agent

MEMORANDUM

TO: Keith

FROM: Bruce

RE: Chapter Nine—Your Church as Change Agent

Dear Keith,

I really enjoyed the extra day we spent in Nevada after the meeting. I don't know if you feel at ease doing it, but I think the things you said about being bored in church services might really be helpful in this chapter. Does the church have to be boring? What **is** the church? How can the church be the salt and the light and what if the salt has lost its savor? These are some of the questions which came to mind after our conversation. I know you have really deep convictions on this subject and I hope you'll pull out all the stops.

It's rained all day here. My car broke down and I have a cold. It's one of those days when I need to remember that God loves me.

Bruce

What Is the Average Church Really Like?

What is the average church actually like? This past year I was visiting the Sunday services of a church I'd never attended. I was feeling grateful to God for a new chance to work and I wanted very much to worship him. When I walked in, the people were not unfriendly, but not particularly friendly either. No one actually spoke, although the usher nodded. I sat in a pew about halfway down the aisle and began to participate in the worship service.

The minister made some announcements and then started to conduct the service, all in a voice obviously reserved for religious occasions. He didn't seem to be particularly enthusiastic or excited about anything he was doing or saying, but was merely reading through the Scripture and the liturgy in a workmanlike manner. We all sat, read our parts, and listened, sang, or knelt on cue. When he got up to preach, the tone didn't vary.

Through the whole service I was having a terrible time concentrating. What he said was not particularly edifying to me, nor challenging, nor poignant. It seemed, in fact, boring. In about five minutes—or it may have been ten—I woke with a start to realize that my mind had been a thousand miles away. I am usually a very good listener and am intensely interested in everything about the Gospel of Jesus Christ, including the process of communicating it.

As I sat there, I thought to myself, "What's wrong with you, Keith? You're not putting any energy in this service. You act like you're bored to death." And I said, "Lord, forgive me. I love you and want to tell you that. But here I am acting as if I were bored. Forgive me!" I thought that maybe, because I am a public speaker and because my subject matter is Christianity, I was just getting to be a cynical professional.

But then suddenly it was as if an inner voice said to me, "Keith, you really *are* bored, and furthermore this is a *very* boring service." I looked around at the other worshipers, and many of them were staring at the preacher with that glassy distant look. It dawned on me that many of them were bored, too. Then I realized something

163

that may be one of the most carefully guarded secrets in the church: thousands of us are very bored when we sit in church, but we don't have the guts to say so. I wanted to stand up and shout it to the congregation.

Maybe nobody wanted to come to this service, including the minister. "Could it be," I thought, "that perhaps millions of other people are bored or find the worship in the average church irrelevant to the needs of their lives and relationships to people? And if this is true, why hasn't somebody *just said it?* Why do we put the blame on ourselves and keep silent? Why don't we just *say* that our needs are not being met through that kind of worship service? We are not even worshiping God with the enthusiasm that we reserve for ordinary other things which are really important to us!"

I realized, as I said these things to God, that we do not help well, that we are not effective agents of change in the world because *we* are not going on any real adventure in the body of Christ to invite people to join. We Christians in the pews are not getting our own lives changed in any deep and significant ways in church nor facing the pain and lostness in our own lives. So we have nothing to take to the people outside the church. Certainly we don't have the desire to go out there with nothing—especially since we don't feel the energy of the presence of God in our midst.

I know the arguments against what I am saying. You may say that I am projecting my own lack of faith on other people. I know that I am being critical and that people will say to me, "You expect too much." I know that others will say, "Everybody is not as enthusiastic as you," or, "We don't always have to have excited feelings." But just the same, I feel strongly that there is something desperately sick and wrong about the average church congregation's worship. And I do not believe we will *ever* change until we *feel* and *express* the frustration, the boredom, and lack of involvement we often experience when we get together as Christians.

The Church Doesn't Have to Be Boring

Between Sundays I am in groups of Christians struggling to be God's people in a very personal, dynamic way. These groups are often filled with adventure and life. We are not bored as we struggle to find out how to survive the pain and anguish of our own sin and try to stay honest with each other when our needs and fears drive us in opposite directions. We are not bored as we face our loneliness, our broken homes, and the reasons they have broken; as we face business failure and what we might do to survive another week; as we examine and pray about our failure with our children, or our struggles to be what we think we should be spiritually, physically, morally, intellectually as we try to help people in the world. It is never boring when we are being real.

As I thought about these things that morning in church, I remembered that in counseling interviews when things get boring, the counselee (or counselor) is hiding something—consciously or unconsciously. And I realized that in the churches where I feel bored, I do not sense any openness from pastors or people. I have the feeling that we are in some way hiding from each other—and are consequently boring.

The New Testament definition of the church centers in the Greek word *ecclesia* (Acts 5:11), meaning "the called-out ones," "those called together."

There is also Paul's vivid analogy of the *church* as a body with different connected members all "organically" alive to the same head—and heart.

So a group of the called-out ones who have been gathered together by the Lord to live our *whole lives*—to work, to pray, to minister and to enjoy life together—make up the church, the body of Christ in any given place. To us has been entrusted the ministry of bringing the broken lost people and situations in the world back together in his body.

As I thought back to the service in which I had been sitting, I could see no evidence that anyone there was trying to change his or her own behavior or relationships *or* working on learning about practicing this ministry of reconciliation. After the service, people didn't speak to me unless I spoke first. And they really didn't talk to each other unless they were obviously pretty good friends. To call that a community of people called out to mend broken relationships and to be on an adventure together would be the most bizarre thing I could imagine. I can't say this hard enough. For my whole lifetime, we have ignored the *enormous* disparity between what is said and what we do in our churches. Either I am insane, or there is some strange conspiracy of silence which will not let us face the fantastic stereotyped charade we go through each Sunday in many churches. We do not come to grips with each other, with our own real problems, with the brokenness and lostness all around us right in the room—much less in the world.

I know there are exceptions to this condition in the church; I know personally of dozens of them. But the fact that we can even call these exceptions is almost unbelievable. I am so sick of my own failure to stand up and face this blight on the body of Christ, I simply cannot stand it any longer. I don't know that I can do anything about it, but I pray to God that someone out there reading this book will hear me and that I or you will have the courage to begin at least to change things in our own lives. Until we in the church become aware that *we* need a physician in our corporate life, even God won't help us. (See Luke 5:31–32.)

When the Salt Has Lost Its Savor

There is a strange deterioration that takes place in all religious movements, which is evidently normal in terms of historical process. Alfred North Whitehead states this pretty clearly when he says, "On the whole, well-established religious institutions are to be reckoned among the conservative forces of society. They soon become the grand support of what Clement had termed 'communal custom'. But the ultimate ideals, of which they profess themselves guardian, are a standing criticism of current practice."[1]

I think this is what has happened to us in the church. We talk about ourselves as having found hope, meaning, and integrity and wanting to share it with the world. We talk about being forgiven and having new starts, but then we live through committee meetings without heart-searching prayer or confession or without honest engagement with each other concerning the pressing problems in our own lives. And we fail to cry out at the things we are doing together which don't seem right. We calmly look at the manipulating of people for evangelistic purposes, to get a large head count of "saved" souls, without ever crying, "*No!* This is a sin against God to manipulate people—even to get them into his kingdom." We look at the sterility of our public worship without even being conscious any more of our boredom and lack of passion and love. Indeed our ultimate ideals are a standing criticism of our current practice.

This disease of complacency and irrelevancy is not limited to the life of the church. In many places our educational, political, and cultural institutions are suffering from the same separation between professed beliefs and practice. And the need to turn and face reality is a boil ready for lancing.

For a long time I have realized that new life in the church follows an awareness of sin, then repentance, and confession. But most of us have not confessed or even seen our sin in this respect *since* our conversion. I have read a lot in the past about "carnal Christians." Having known much failure and frustration in my life, I've been saying to myself, "Who am I to stand up and point out to the church that we are boring and uninteresting to the world and even to ourselves?" But now I realize that *whoever* says these things, confessing our sin, has got to be somebody imperfect. God doesn't *have any perfect* people to speak to or for the church.

When I say there are no *perfect* Christians to speak out for God or be his change agents, I am not talking about the occasional church-goer or the peripheral member. I am talking about Sunday school superintendents, pastors in their pulpits, all kinds of church officers, missionaries, the ordinary, average, earnest Christians. As Oswald Chambers said, "We are nice people; you would love to meet some of us." Some of us even know how to talk the language of Christianity and salvation and mean every word we say. We are not hypocrites. But a lot of us are tired, desperately tired. I talk to Christians all the time who seem overwhelmed inwardly with the sense of defeat, frustration, futility, and barrenness in terms of their attempts to work and live in the body of Christ.

Jesus described us in our lethargy and fear of being honest when he said, "If the salt has lost its taste, how shall its saltness be restored? It is no longer good for anything except to be thrown out and trodden underfoot by men" (Matt. 5:13). And that's what's happening to the church in many places.

How Can the Flavor Be Restored?

What keeps new life from breaking out and maturing in the average congregation? Although I am a professional and have held leadership positions in the church, I still must say that I believe we professionals and leaders are the primary blocks to new life in the church. I realize that in many places the congregations do not want to come alive and that they are not converted to Jesus Christ. But that is no excuse.

Many, many times the reason that new life can't flourish when it does break out is the subtle squelching or careful manipulative control of that new life by lay and clerical leaders in the church, who do not trust change unless they can control it. I don't think this squelching is intentional nor do I think it is even conscious always. The leaders I know would probably say that they are "protecting the congregation from irrational outbursts and from the naïveté of new Christians." But I think this is a very uncreative and unrealistic view of the process of change in the body of Christ.

As one who is called a leader, I feel that I must listen to and be willing to consider *any* change and take the insights of other lay people very seriously. I must remember that *they* have a relationship with God which may be in many ways more direct than mine, since it is new and fresh and is sometimes the result of an unreserved commitment. But this is very threatening. I know a little about the agony contemporary clergymen face in terms of their own identity and authenticity. If lay men and women can come up with new ideas to change the church and can bring new life and adventure into the parish when the minister can't, who *is* the minister and what is he for?

So the choice sometimes becomes that of protecting and controlling the church's activities so that he will have a place for himself or herself that has meaning and authority. But if ministers and lay leaders don't become open to new life and enthusiasm in the mainline churches, then the hope of those churches becoming effective agents of change in our kind of world is almost nil. Because somehow the same passionate new life and adventure that are brought into the congregation by excited Christians are the vehicles on which change and the Holy Spirit will eventually ride into the pain and lostness of the world.

It seems that ministers must make a choice that emotionally they are going to be with the people who are committed to life—whether or not those are the people with money and prestige. This does not mean a desertion of such people who are not interested in new life. It means that one cannot serve two masters nor can he ride two horses. Sooner or later, if the new life is to mature, he must tell the people in the new life group, "I am with you. I am a part of you. I don't know what is going to happen, but I believe in you and I will support you." He can also continue to try to minister to the traditional power people in the church who are not involved, and they may get rid of him. But as we said earlier, a passionate new group cannot thrive and grow in the Christian adventure unless its leaders are not only in favor of them but somehow *on the adventure with them* with their own lives and vulnerability.

I understand a little about the practical difficulties of what I am suggesting—that people in the average congregation simply will not participate and take leadership roles with the enthusiasm and intense interest I am describing. But I am not talking about the average congregation. I am talking about the body of Christ as represented by those who are personally committed to go on the adventure with him, those who have committed their whole lives to the finding and doing of his will for them and for the world. Many of us professionals are making a good living out of our telling other people to "risk all" to follow Christ. But the people will never really change until *we* risk it all. And when I say this seriously, it scares me to death, because I'm afraid I can't do it.

The change-agent groups are paradoxical. The ones who are really powerful are often not seen to be. The New Testament images of God's church are things like "salt" and "yeast." Both of these are agents which cause change through a very intimate contact with the substance being changed. The basic transformation takes place because of the *nature of the change agents*—which incidentally don't call attention to themselves. Yeast, for instance, can change an entire loaf of bread in a very visible way without the world being able to see the *crucial* action happening. The action of salt is also invisible.

And I believe that the power for changing society comes through these intimate adventuring bands of Christians who are sensitized carriers of an "invisible spirit" to whom they are committed in purpose and in love. I know of nowhere else where the world can find a medicine comparable to that of a community of people who are hilariously free because they have seen something of the depths of their sin and selfishness and been forgiven. We Christians who have confession, forgiveness, and new chances built into the fabric of all we do and are, do not have to back off from problems and take our succeeding so seriously—because we can risk making mistakes. And I believe it is only the committed group that becomes an agent of change which can transform persons and institutions in society through its presence and contact at the point of pain.

After twenty years of experience, I laugh at people who tell me that it is dangerous to turn the church over to untrained laymen. In the first place I know now from twenty years of studying theology that the Christian faith and life are not all that precise. *No one* knows much about how to live the Christian life really well, and even fewer people can. The ones whose record seems best to me— those who seem to live closest to God and to take the time to love other people—are in many cases untrained lay persons who are deeply committed to Jesus Christ. They often outlove us professionals, they outperform us, they outgive us, and they do these things without the three or four years of professional training we have—and without the remuneration we receive for our work. These are frightening statements. And I find myself afraid that I will be ostracized because of having written them. But I believe they are true.

Change Agent Groups Become "Family" in a New Way

One of the fascinating things about the body of Christ when we are people on an adventure dealing with real pain and lostness is that the differences which ordinarily separate us in social and vocational situations can fade into insignificance. And we may become brothers and sisters, instead of highly stratified members of an organization. Philip Yancey gives us a poignant picture of this phenomenon in describing a visit to the intensive care ward in a hospital. There the rich, poor, black, white, smart, and dull are all united by a single awful threat—their love for a dying relative or friend. Often they will be consoling each other or crying quietly. And in Christian churches on the adventure this same closeness and intimacy often become the natural way life together is.

One of the strange phenomena of the church's history is that when we get very far away from this adventure with the living Christ and begin to have quietly controlled services and activities for ourselves, the awareness of the Holy Spirit simply departs. We are left with beautiful church buildings, along with our tranquil, perfect worship forms. But we no longer experience the energy and spirit of the Lord.

The Holy Spirit, it seems, comes to us and gives us strength to be change agents, when we need it and cry out for him. In most of our churches we don't *need* God's strength to do what we are already doing. We can conduct the services, the meetings of the men and women of the church, the vestry meetings, and the every-member canvass simply by having enough bodies present which are motivated to keep the organization going for the good of the group.

But when we face blinding failure with each other and people in the world, senseless catastrophes, failures, and broken marriages, terrified fears of the future—when we face these things together, we *must* pray for strength and guidance from the Holy Spirit. And amazingly, *that* is when he brings these things into our life together—when we can't do the job ourselves. And he brings creative solutions we never would have thought of ahead of time. Sometimes he just brings experience and pain for us too, so that we can live with hurting people and let them feel the closeness of the Holy Spirit in us as we allow them to sée our own helplessness and yet our hope in Christ.

The Healing Salt May Also Have a Sting

Besides bringing love into the pain and lostness of the world, I believe that a biblical faith demands that, as change agents, we Christians are also to bring justice. But biblical justice is not justice in the sense we ordinarily think of it.

Many people think about justice as "absolute equality." For example, if I am standing in a line for food in America, I have a right to my place; and if justice prevails, I can hold my place and no one can take it away from me. But if I am a Christian living on the adventure with God, I may see justice as giving up my place to a tired and hungry older person who might not be able to wait out the line for food. That would be Christ's sort of justice. And it is a kind of justice the world knows very little about. And when we in the church want to go into the world as God's change agents to "do justice," we cannot look only to the legal code as guide but must look beyond it to the law of love. That's one of the reasons we need to "practice" God's sort of justice with each other in our own groups on the adventure. Only as we experience this will we have some notion of how to make decisions to implement his kind of loving justice in the world. If we simply try to go out and do the "fair thing," we will give only short-term help. Because the "fair thing," strangely, does not often have in it the explosive seeds for the dramatic changes needed in society.

It is somehow the extravagant justice from passionate people that unlocks hostile hearts, closed doors, and knotty situations. It has become increasingly apparent to me that learning how to love and how to mediate justice are matters which by their very nature must be learned in personal community. We simply have to have experiences of second-mile love and of justice before we can mediate these things to other people with any kind of sensitivity.

There is no set rule or foolproof way I know of that a church can become an agent of change. As I've suggested, I think it is the natural outcome of the process of being Christian adventurers together, trying to find and do God's will. The Holy Spirit eventually sensitizes us to the pain in the world—when we have gained some security through the loving strength of Christ as he heals our own pain and guides us in changing our lives.

The church can be a powerful change-agent in society if we begin by letting him change the changers: us.

MEMORANDUM

TO: Bruce

FROM: Keith

RE: Chapter Nine—Your Church as Change Agent

Dear Bruce,

I'm really glad my section of this chapter is behind me. It has been the hardest chapter to write for me. I've had kind of a love/hate relationship with the church for years. I get impatient, critical, and restless. But then I realize again and again that the church is my only home and family in some ways. I've been afraid to express some of my feelings in print until now. I was afraid ministers and deeply involved lay people would reject me and what I was saying. But now that I am convinced that there is no hope for Christianity to exist and flourish outside some form of the church, I'm ready to try to face the music, roll up my sleeves, and deal with some of the pressing problems I see in our being a change agent church.

But there is much hope in the church and many effective congregations who are being effective change agents. Why don't you show us what you see happening and point to some of the life and positive action you see?

Bruce, what do you see as God's message to and through us in the church? How has the church been on the forefront of change? What can we dream at this time in history? Can you give some examples of contemporary change agent churches? And finally, is there a certain level or a common way all change agent churches could see this mission?

Hope things are going well with you. I'm busy but doing fine! I'm enjoying Waco. Hope you can come to visit soon.

Keith

I n this book we are considering how we can best be change agents for God's new order. Should we "lose our lives for Christ and his Kingdom" only within the confines of the organized church? Or, finding the church irrelevant in many areas, should we find other avenues for being agents of God's will in the world? These are heavy questions.

It's easy to be sentimental about the church, as was the author of these lines:

> There shall always be the Church and the World,
> And the heart of man
> Shivering and fluttering between them choosing and chosen,
> Valiant, ignoble, dark, and full of life
> Swinging between hell gate and Heaven gate
> And the gates of hell shall not prevail.

But while most of us are stirred by such sentimental feelings about the church, it is also easy to be critical about it. Our experience provides the grounds for both emotions. One of the more pessimistic stories about the nature of the church that made a lasting impression on me comes from Howard Thurman, Dean of Chapel at Boston University while I was doing graduate work there. One Sunday, he told the story of a man on a journey who came to a town where no one wore shoes. It was winter time and all the residents had blue and frozen feet, in some cases bleeding from the ice and snow. The visitor asked the manager of the hotel where he was staying what the practice meant. "What practice?" was the retort. The visitor pointed to the man's bare feet. "Why isn't anyone in this town wearing shoes? Don't you believe in shoes?"

"Believe in shoes, my friend! I should say we do. A belief in shoes is the first article in our creed. They are indispensable to the well-being of humanity. They prevent chilblains, cuts, sores, and suffering." "Well, why don't you wear them?" asked the traveler. "Ah," responded the manager, "that's just it. Why don't we?"

Later walking around the town the visitor inquired about a huge building he saw. "That is one of our outstanding shoe manufacturing establishments," he was told. "You mean you make shoes there?" asked the newcomer in amazement. "Well, not exactly," was the answer. "We talk about making shoes there and we have hired a most brilliant young fellow to speak on the subject every week. Just yesterday he moved his hearers so profoundly that they broke down and wept. It was wonderful!" "But why don't you wear shoes?" the stranger asked insistently. "Ah," the townsman said. "That's just it. Why don't we?"

In Thurman's story the man finally comes upon a cobbler making shoes in a little basement shop. He rushes in and buys three pairs as a gift for his new friend. The friend was embarrassed. "Ah, thank you." he said politely. "But you don't understand. It just isn't done. The first families don't wear them."

As Howard Thurman's whimsical story suggests, all too often the church advocates a way of life everyone believes in but no one practices.

Defining the Church

But before we can accept or reject the church as our place of ministry we must first ask: what is the church? Of course there is no static answer. In describing the church we are like the blind men who came upon an elephant and attempted to describe it. One grabbed the tail and said, "An elephant is like a rope." A second grabbed the leg, hugged it and said, "An elephant is like a tree." Another bumped into the solid flank of the elephant and said, "An elephant is like a wall." Still another got hold of the tusks and said, "An elephant is like stone." Each man was right and each was wrong.

Basically the church is a worshiping community of people committed to Jesus Christ in any given time or place. Because each Christian person is different, each grouping becomes a different and unique cluster within the corporate whole. But throughout history there have been those Christians who have understood the nature of the church and that its mission is to include the whole of society—in other words the "boundaries" of the church and society as a whole are eventually to be the same.

But besides the different boundaries of the church, there are differences in the way people hear what God says to his church. The comforting secure words of the Twenty-third Psalm are just one part of the biblical message. By contrast God says through Jeremiah, "Thus says the Lord: Behold, what I have built I am breaking down, and what I have planted I am plucking up—that is, the whole land. And do you seek great things for yourself? Seek them not; for, behold, I am bringing evil upon all flesh, says the Lord; but I will give you your life as a prize of war in all places to which you may go" (45:4–5, RSV).

This God is the God of change. He not only threatens to destroy the evil works of men, he also proclaims that even his own works will be uprooted in order to do a new thing in our time. And the church throughout the ages has been the most powerful change agent for human society that the world has ever seen. Most of the great revolutionary advances in man's corporate life in the Western world have come about through those who have believed in the gospel of Jesus Christ and who have become the church in action.

The Church in the Forefront of Change

The church at its best has been responsible for establishing hospitals, orphanages, asylums—for promoting equal rights under the law, prison reform, child labor laws, and the franchise for all people. As we reflect on the revolutionary new concepts which have been released in society, some of the great names of the church come to mind.

The church is St. Francis of Assisi, whose whole style of life dramatized the need for the people of God to care for the sick, the lepers, the poor, and the outcasts, and to revere nature.

The church is John Calvin, who by putting the Christian faith into theological and political form in Geneva, Switzerland, modeled the representative form of government we practice today. These same radical political concepts spread into Hungary, Germany, France, and Scotland. Wherever the Reformed faith of the Calvinists spread, education and political freedom followed. Kitchen maids in Geneva under Calvin or in Scotland under John Knox could read and write at a time when even most courtiers of other lands could not. Scotland became the first truly literate country, complete with schools for all ages. And when the Calvinist Puritan fathers came to America, their first concern was to build schools. All of the earliest American colleges were formed by churchmen.

The church is Dwight Moody, who, apart from being one of the great evangelists of all time, started schools for the poor, rural girls and boys of Northfield, Massachusetts. These schools still continue and flourish. This great evangelist had a passion to provide education for the poor and the underprivileged. It was Charles Finney, another great evangelist, whose concern for education led to the founding of Oberlin College.

The church is John and Charles Wesley, who communicated the love of God to the common people of England and laid the groundwork for a social reformation which historians credit with saving England from a bloody revolution. Their preaching, their prayer meetings, and the education of their converts through the Wesleyan class meeting changed the structure of English society in one generation. This early Methodist church brought public education, the voting franchise, the abolition of slavery, the passage of labor laws and the establishment of orphanages and hospitals.

The church is Father Damien, a Roman Catholic priest and missionary, who brought aid and loving care to the lepers at Molokai, Hawaii. The church through Father Damien brought hope, help and healing to a previously hopeless and outcast segment of society.

The church is Martin Luther King, Jr., who spearheaded the civil rights movement in the United States. This Baptist minister stood squarely in the tradition of the church and used his powers as a minister of the gospel to lead one of the great social reforms of our time.

There are hundreds of examples of the people of God permeating the mainstream of history with much needed renewal and change.

The Church with a Dream

Now, all of this does not mean that all churches everywhere are concerned about being change agents in society. As a matter of fact, it is frequently the church which seems to thwart particular members who try to act in a radical way in terms of social or personal change. But at the same time, I believe there are those forces in the church in every age who will join in the liberating ministry to which God has called his people. I remember hearing the Bishop of Toronto say a few years ago to some of his congregation, "God does not spend much time in church!" His is the kind of leadership which produces those caring Christians who are determined to be God's change agents in the world.

I believe this is a special time for dreams and visions for us Christians. While the major structures of our society appear to be falling apart, it is possible that this is the very time for building. Like the Israelites who returned from captivity to find their homeland in ruin, we also may have a chance to start over to build a city or society under God the way he meant it to be. It is my profound belief that there are countless passionate Christians in many churches all across the world who have that dream of building with and for God.

I believe that we cannot separate the church's ministry in terms of evangelism from its ministry of comfort and healing or from its mission to be involved in the world for God's sake. All three somehow go together.

The Church in the Marketplace

My mother is a remarkable Christian and has been for most of her life. When my stepfather died, she was eighty-one. Loneliness, grief and self-pity seemed to overwhelm her. Months went by and the situation got no better though she read her Bible and prayed morning and night.

Finally, one of her pastors asked her to help in a new program offering tutoring help to grade school children in a nearby black ghetto. Since she is a former teacher she accepted, though she was decades older than any of the other volunteer tutors. She was assigned a fifth grader named Rosemary with whom she began to work on a regular basis.

Almost immediately all of us saw a change in my mother. In giving herself sacrificially to someone who needed her, she found a new channel for her love and concern. Through Rosemary, God gave my mother the consolation and strength to heal her own wounds and grief. This simply underlines for me the fact that beyond worship and prayer and Bible study and a genuinely pious life, we Christians must be involved in the needs of the world for *our own well-being and growth*. The church in its truest essence must be rooted in the needs, hurts and pain of society. The authentic church and the healthy church is the church in the marketplace helping, healing and liberating.

Some Contemporary Change-Agents

This kind of church honestly and unselfconsciously involved in life beyond its own walls, continues to have tremendous power. It has, of course, spiritual power which is the mark of the Holy Spirit indwelling and infilling his people. But beyond that it is a secular, political and cultural force.

For years the Hollywood Presbyterian Church has been a model for changing lives within its surrounding community. As is true of so many of our inner-city churches, it is located in an area that has deteriorated seriously in recent years. One of the problems confronting the church was a proliferation of massage parlors in the immediate vicinity. Determined to curb this depressing situation, concerned laymen began their campaign by bringing about changes in the licensing of these establishments. Stringent rules were established. For example, anyone who operated a massage parlor had to have a significant prescribed number of hours of training in professional massage. In other words, a massage parlor had to be a real massage parlor.

In addition, members of the Hollywood congregation are working on the problems of prostitution and drug peddling in the neighborhood. They have even begun to buy up many of the surrounding buildings which were previously used for illicit purposes and have turned them into low cost housing for the elderly. The church continues to minister in the name of Jesus to individuals who need to grow spiritually, but it has enlarged its ministry to become a change agent in its own neighborhood and community.

All Saints Episcopal Church in Jacksonville, Florida, is another church functioning in its true biblical role. Its members are tithers, prayers, and supporters of many worthwhile causes. In recent years they have established a school for retarded preschool children on their church campus. It is the only school of its kind I know of, secular or sacred, in the entire state of Florida. They are pioneers in providing a new kind of care for a needy group of children.

Perhaps one of the best-known change-agent churches is The Church of The Saviour in Washington, D.C. Many lives have been changed by Jesus Christ in and through that church. One of their newest projects, Jubilee Housing, involves buying slum housing, renovating and selling the buildings at below cost to needy families. This unusual church, which has already made such an impact on the spiritual and moral life of people, is now a change agent for housing in one of the slum areas of our nation's capitol. It is an impressive ministry for a church which over the years has seldom had more than one hundred active members at any given time.

A Mission on Many Levels

Are most of us in our churches functioning as effective change agents in today's world? Probably not. In thinking of the mission of the church, imagine a father with five children. As he's sitting in his easy chair one evening, one child runs up crying, "Daddy, I hurt my finger. Please kiss it and make it better." A little later a second child comes into the room. "Dad, I'm working on a very important project and I need money," he says. "Could I have an advance on my allowance?" Before long a third child comes in with a different request, "Dad, could you help me with my homework? I'm stuck on one problem." Near the end of the evening the youngest child comes quietly down the stairs and crawls into Daddy's lap. "What can I do for you, child?" asks the father. The answer is, "Nothing. I just want to be near you and love you." Finally when all four of the younger children are in bed, the oldest child comes in to talk. "Father, I was talking to some friends today about the work your committee is doing to help some of the disadvantaged people in our town. We'd like to know if you could use our help."

Which of the children does the father love most? The father loves them all. He was able to give a different kind of help to each one of his five children out of his love and according to their particular needs.

It seems to me we could liken the Christian church to this family of children. Because of our own needs, hurts, or problems, each of us perceives God in a different way. This perception affects our manner of worship and our sense of service or lack of it. I'm coming to believe that the various emphases in our different churches do not so much reflect the nature of our theological concepts of God as the conscious needs and discoveries of people.

But Christian maturity for the church as well as for each of its members comes with the discovery that God is more than the supplier of all of our needs. He is the restless, creative, redeeming, building God who is at work in his creation through the lives and affairs of people. But while we are privileged to join him in this work of creation and re-creation, we must not forget that we are also dependent children. We never outgrow our need for his comfort, his healing, his illumination of our minds, his provision for our daily needs or for his love.

Chapter Ten

The Cost of Loving

MEMORANDUM

TO: Keith

FROM: Bruce

RE: Chapter Ten—The Cost of Loving

Dear Keith,

I feel like this next chapter is especially challenging for both of us, since we originally wanted to title this book "The Cost of Adventure." I know our publishers felt that title had rather negative and even scary connotations for most people. And perhaps they were right. We're all a little leery of getting into a venture that will really cost us something.

Why don't you make this a starting point for your section: Exactly what is the cost of loving? Does it feel sacrificial? In what way will our lives be affected—both negatively and positively?

There is a wonderful southwest wind up just now. I wish you were here to go sailing.

Bruce

When I've heard about Christians who have made a "total commitment to Christ" and "given up" comfortable lives to "do God's will," I've often wondered how they could pay such a cost, could make such sacrifices. But I now believe that my reaction involves a very basic misunderstanding of the kind of sacrifice we call the "cost of discipleship."

When I was growing up, a popular song warned that you'd better watch out because "the love bug might bite you"—you might fall in love. And if you were bitten, you sort of lost your sanity. You found yourself doing things you never thought you'd do to make your loved one happy. I don't remember how the lyrics went, but having been through the experience of falling in love, I know that the song expresses a real truth.

I realize now that I was a very selfish young man, in many ways. I resented any encroachment on my time away from my personal activities (like moping around the house or playing basketball). And I was not exactly known for spending money on other people. Then in high school I fell in love, and a great transformation took place in my life. I got a job to earn money, and I couldn't wait to get through basketball practice so I could go over to my girlfriend's house and take her flowers (or in one case a gold necklace which I spent my savings to buy). The world was sweet and new. Nothing seemed too much to do or to get for my true love. I'd put aside everything I'd held dear a month before, but I was hardly experiencing what people think of as a life of sacrifice. And yet in a real sense I was. I had renounced those things which had seemed most important for me: my moody solitude, my preoccupation with sports, and the exclusive claim on my money. And it all seemed perfectly natural, given my new focus: Mary. My parents thought I'd gone crazy.

And according to the way most people think about the process of commitment and the renunciation it demands, I should have been miserable. But in fact, if you had questioned me I would not have thought I had given up *anything*. I'd probably just have looked at you as if *you* were crazy, since I knew that I had chosen a relationship with the most wonderful girl in the world. As a result of this choosing and being with my girlfriend, I had just made a *different set of choices* about how I was going to spend my time and money. But I *wanted* to do these things because I had *chosen* to. As a matter of fact being with Mary was all I thought about doing.

I think this is a pretty fair analogy of what happens when we make a serious personal commitment to Christ and his people. Our use of time and money change drastically, sometimes overnight, sometimes over a period of months or years. But the new adventurer does not think he is living a grim life of renunciation at all. He is suddenly in a love relationship with a Lord he wants to get to know and to live for and with some exciting new friends. He has come alive, and instead of giving only intellectual assent to a doctrine, he has become passionate about God and the love of people. This is something of the strange phenomenon which is like falling in love and which happens when people are confronted with a call to give "their whole lives" to God.

The problem is often that we preach about the necessity of sacrificial giving and renunciation of selfish pursuits to people who may have joined a church but never consciously and specifically stepped into a committed love relationship with God which involved their whole lives. Imagine a parent *demanding* that his teenage boy give up his solitude and basketball and use his money for a girl with whom he had *not* fallen in love—and hoping he would decide on his own to do this.

What I am trying to say is that when one really tries to give himself in a commitment to Christ and his people, then renunciation doesn't seem like sacrifice at all. Some of the greatest men and women in history have discovered this fact. Louis Fischer describes Ghandi's feelings: "With faith, renunciation is not sacrifice. It substitutes one pleasure for another. Some give a donation, Ghandi gave himself— and found himself. The amount of giving is determined by the intensity of belief. 'Only give up a thing,' Ghandi wrote, 'when you want some other conditions so much that the thing has no longer any attraction for you, or when it seems to interfere with that which is more greatly desired.' "[1]

So one of the secrets of the passionate people is that we are not making a sacrifice as the world thinks of sacrifice. We are in fact choosing a way of life which leads to a joy and fulfillment hitherto unknown to us. Many of the missionaries who went back to Africa after their friends and families had been attacked and murdered were thought to be fanatically religious. But when one talked to such people, they *wanted to* go back. They did not feel like great heroes. Somehow the condition of being in Africa and the fulfillment they found when they were working there meant more to them than the dangers they might face or the security they could have by staying safely in a quiet job in the United States.

I remember as a young boy being afraid of getting kicked in the face playing football. The day came that I got on a team and was playing with a bunch of boys whose love and respect I really wanted. In the excitement of the game and in the sense of being together with them in a common cause, I remember forgetting my fear and tackling a very large boy all by myself. I did in fact get kicked very hard as I tackled him, but somehow the pain was muted because of the exhilaration of making the tackle. I am sure the impact was no less than it would otherwise have been, but because I was committed to the team and to the effort we were all making together, there was a higher value than my own safety which came into play and I hardly noticed the pain. And I quite willingly threw my body at this boy—as a matter of fact I rushed to do it. To an onlooking child this might have looked like a great act of heroism. But to me, being a part of the game, it was the natural and inevitable thing to do, because I was on the field and on the team. I think there is a strong resemblance between the attitude I am describing and that of a Christian on God's adventure in the world.

But a "life of sacrifice" is not a series of dramatic decisions in which one decides whether to go to Africa or not. It begins as a "local" commitment to give one's self to Christ and his people for the finding and doing of God's will—believing that he has in mind for us wholeness and joy. In other words, we trust God that if we will do what we know of his will where we are, he will give us understanding, completeness, and build our souls, characters, and vocations into their creative and happy potential.

Is This Call to Recommitment Realistic?

Talk of this kind of "total commitment" or recommitment may sound terribly naïve to the average church lay leader or even pastor who has tried to drum up enthusiasm for worthy programs. But it is simply *not* true that people will not *want* to try to make a "total commitment (or recommitment) to God," if they hear it can be tried realistically. We are almost never seriously *asked* to make that kind of commitment in any case. It's not that we are called to commit too much in the average church. We aren't asked to commit *enough*. And consequently most of us are neither hot nor cold.

When I was wrestling with whether to try to recommit my whole life to Jesus Christ after my faith had mysteriously eroded several years ago, I realized something I'd never seen before: when I was converted twenty years before, I had tried to give my whole life to God. But I saw that many of the things and people which are very important to me *now* in my life *were not even included in that earlier commitment!* My writing and speaking were not included—I hadn't done any. The material things I have acquired since then were not included. And some very important relationships—like that with my youngest daughter, with Andrea, and with Bruce and Hazel— were not part of my "total commitment to Christ" of twenty years ago.

As I realized these things I saw that hundreds of thousands of us in the church may be feeling smug and "totally committed to Christ" when in fact much of our life and many of our relationships have been given to us *since* we came into God's family. I was deeply confronted. Was I willing to recommit my life, *including* putting God before my new relationships, my writing, my material security? I didn't know. I was afraid to turn loose again and ashamed of my fear. And in the writing of this book I have been wrestling with this commitment at a new level: am I willing to move outside of myself and into the brokenness and lostness of the world as I am feeling called to do?

There is a sense in which Jesus Christ has always demanded an absolute allegiance to himself and to God's will. It may be that no one can fulfill that allegiance, but as William Temple said, "Absoluteness of allegiance is the very life-breath of religion." Of course that doesn't mean that no one can properly be called a Christian who doesn't have this absolute allegiance, but it is essential to wholeness and the hope for new life in the church that we should all regard God as entitled to such total commitment and ourselves as under an obligation to give it. If we are going to be God's passionate people and carriers of his caring love into the pain of the world we must have this true allegiance as our conscious goal. We may not be able to make the "total commitment" a reality except in fleeting moments. But what we can do is to tell God that we are "willing to be made willing" to give him our total allegiance, and then begin the next chapter of the adventure as a reality on that basis. It is in this context that God calls us to specific tasks and that the renunciation and changing of crippling possessions and habits may take place, which will allow us to become carriers of the Spirit of the living God into the pain of the world.

The Place of Discipline

Even though the Christian life is the happiest I've known, paradoxically it is not easy and it takes a lot of discipline for me to stay at it. The whole thing is a paradox: it's easy, and yet it's incredibly hard, to be a committed Christian. But there comes a time when one just realizes that it is worth the price in time and energy to live a disciplined life with God. And then it may become enjoyable in a new way.

Several years ago I was feeling very sluggish physically and wasn't sleeping well. I went through an outstanding medical clinic in Houston, Texas. When I had completed the tests the doctor sat me down and said, "Keith, medically there isn't anything seriously wrong with you, but unless you change your style of living somehow, you may die in a very few years." He suggested I take some time off and that I begin to jog and take exercises every day.

I didn't "have time" to jog and do exercises, but the doctor's announcement caused me to make a commitment and to begin.

When I first began to jog and to exercise—things I used to hate because they were so boring—I gasped for breath, my legs were sore, and I wanted to give up at every opportunity. But because of what the doctor had said, I kept on. Then one day I began to feel better. I wasn't gasping for breath, my leg muscles began to feel firm and I started to sleep soundly. I became aware that I wasn't as irritable with the people around me as I had been. My relationships were more open and direct, and I thought more clearly. And in the months and years which followed, a change has taken place which I never would have believed: *I love to jog!* I can smell the earth in the mornings. When I am on a beach or area where I can run barefooted, I do. To feel the water and the sand under my feet and to smell the salt, these things are like emotional or spiritual vitamins, permeating my soul and getting me back in touch with life, nature, myself, and with God.

Now, the "cost" of getting in condition does not seem anguishing at all (most mornings) because I'm enjoying the new sense of aliveness I feel. And even the process of exercising has "lost its sting."

What does this have to do with the cost of Christian helping? I think a spiritual process, similar to the physical one I have described, may take place in a Christian's experience with regard to discipline.

For me, the experience of recommitment to Christ was very much like my beginning to jog and do exercises. At first I started changing my behavior because I felt so bad I had to. I joined a small prayer group and began to have a few minutes alone with God in the mornings. In the beginning, facing myself again was very painful—and I wanted to quit. After all, I was a professional Christian who'd written half a dozen books about living the Christian life. But eventually life started to look better. The love and forgiveness I received from God through the small group members gave me strength and motivation to continue the process of getting my spiritual life back in shape. Finally, *after months* of self-centered introspection, confession, and new insights about myself and life, I began to feel good about my relationships with people and with God. And I began to enjoy the disciplines. Now I don't ever like to miss the space I've carved out of my mornings to be alone with God or the small group meetings I attend. And it was at this point that I started to be conscious of *other people's* needs and to help some of them. And the idea was born for my part of this book.

Now I'm convinced more than ever that seriously helping other people effectively *begins* with the cost of committing our own lives to God and beginning (or beginning again) the discipline of learning to live honestly for him and with his people.

We Are Sent into the Real World and Experience Real Agony

Too often we in the churches use the modern techniques of advertising to draw people to us, implying that if they become Christians they will succeed or "be blessed" in all their efforts, that in fact this is God's purpose for us. Such people imply that there will be no darkness and emptiness, no desolation on the Christian way if one is close to Christ and has the Holy Spirit. But that fits neither the facts of the Bible nor those of the greatest Christian lives in the church's history. No, periodically there will always be problems, doubts, and agony for Christ's followers.

It is true that if one really commits his whole future to Christ, there is often a period of enormous release. It has been compared to a sheep submitting itself to the care of a loving shepherd. Anxiety naturally diminishes. I remember feeling, "This is the peace I've dreamed of! I can work hard, but since I don't have to doubt my ultimate succeeding, I can rest when I'm not working. And since I'm in God's hands forever, if I get hurt it won't be 'fatal' in the long-range sense."

But this is only part of the truth. The Bible does not just tell us we are sheep. We are also sons of God and brothers of Christ. And if we grow and stand for God's values in society and in the church, we will be rejected and hurt in unexpected ways. And we will have spiritual failures as long as we are human. And even if we can remember at such times that we are sheep cared for by the good shepherd, it is still scary when the wolves and bears attack from outside and inside our lives. And there *will* be failures and long, dry periods when we wonder if we are insane for having gone on this Christian adventure and renounced other ways of living in our past. At those points we can find great help from our honest brother and sister Christians who have experienced similar things and begun again. The corporate nature of the family of God means, among other things, that when one person's passion for God breaks out anew, it starts an epidemic of new faith within the lives of the rest of us who have become lukewarm or discouraged. Also the manner in which we bear our burdens along the way often releases a power in the Christian family which helps other people become willing to carry on with courage in difficult situations. But our *seeing these things* in real life depends on the open windows in our brothers' and sisters' lives—and our own.

No, I do not think God's long-range purpose in Christ is the life of a victorious sheep singing praises and munching safely in the care of the good shepherd—though I'm ashamed to say I've lived a good bit of my life as if I thought that were true. But we are also called to go out and love the wolves and the bears—or at least those who have been captured by them. And though it will be hard it will have meaning. And meaning, not security, is what separates us from the sheep!

On this journey I am beginning to find the fulfillment I dreamed of in other ways as I move toward becoming one of God's change agents in his bleeding world. And I feel deeply that it is on this adventure with him that we may someday satisfy the restless longing for the fullness of God as we try to live in his way. As Oswald Chambers put it, "We are apt to imagine that if Jesus Christ constrains us, and we obey Him, He will lead us to great success. We must never put our dreams of success as God's purpose for us: His purpose may be exactly the opposite. We have an idea that God is leading us to a particular end, a desired goal: He is not. The questions of getting to a particular end is a mere incident. What we call the process, God calls the end."[2]

The Cost of Discipleship

But having said that there will be pain and difficulties in the way, I do not believe that these difficulties constitute what people on the adventure refer to as the "cost of being a Christian." No, these problems of relating, discipline and finding meaning are *universal* problems. They are the conditions of being *alive*. And the extra burdens and frustrations one may have because he has joined the Christian family are merely the result of trading some of the anguish and pain in the "jungle of the lost" from which we come into God's adventure for some new problems and disciplines. And because of the benefits of receiving forgiveness, hope, and meaning for our lives, we make this trade gladly.

In fact for the committed Christian, none of the universal experiences of pain, failure, and sin are wasted. When we fail to do or be what we want to, that failure and the suffering which follows, can be the occasion for profound future progress in the Christian life. A forgiven sin or painful experience can become like fertilizer for the next period of growth and development.

No, the *"cost"* of being a *Christ-like lover* has more to do with *our willingness to be open, to repent, to confess our sins and make restitution.* And because we can confess in a close group, we can receive love, acceptance and the grace to go on with Christ with a clean mind. And when we surrender our pride enough to give up our battle with guilt and the fear of being known and turn to Jesus Christ, we have paid the cost of entry into the community of the consciously forgiven. And then we may begin to hear what God can teach us through our failures or sins. And we may begin to see the other screwed-up people in the world as our brothers and sisters.

Sometimes when I fail to be Christ's person I get discouraged and want to give up. But this too has been the experience of Christians since the beginning. The "cost" at this point is to get up and go on in faith until some motivational energy takes over, which it does. It's almost like a second wind for a runner.

Anyone who has been involved in a demanding sport knows that there are periods when one's mind and body scream to be released, to quit, to go home and rest. But only those who go through those periods by virtue of some kind of commitment understand the sport and the fulfillment it brings. And a similar road lies ahead of the new or renewed Christian.

Discipleship Means Joy

I am not advising anyone to be paranoid or to look for trouble or agony. I think the best thing to do is to have a great time together looking for God's will and enjoying his world with our fellow adventurers. But I think it is good to know that if we make a serious commitment to Christ and his passionate people, we have left the arena of the innocuous and entered the realm of pain and lostness. And neither the world nor the devil will welcome our entry into these areas. And I have never known a sensitive Christian on this adventure who did not have inner and outer struggles.

But if we answer this call to commitment, what *will* the cost be? Where will it lead and what will happen to us? Dietrich Bonhoeffer said, "To answer this question we shall have to go to Him for only He knows the answer. Only Jesus Christ, who bids us follow Him, knows the journey's end. But we do know that it will be a road of boundless mercy. Discipleship means joy."[3]

MEMORANDUM

TO: Bruce

FROM: Keith

RE: Chapter Ten—The Cost of Loving

Dear Bruce,

Please use the illustrations you told me about last night! I especially love the one about the lion tamer.

Bruce, what do you see as the relationship between doing God's will and paying the cost? What do we have in the way of biblical and historical models when we consider the cost of going ahead on the adventure? How about today in your own experience? What kind of call can God give us which will make us **want** to pay the price to follow Christ? And what kind of support do we have as Christians when we go out alone and risk our lives for him?

Writing and reading this material is really getting to me. Our first two readers may get more out of it than anyone else.

Keith

Many years ago, when I had just become a Christian, I met someone who had a profound effect on my life. He was the pastor of a large Presbyterian church in Sarasota, Florida, and the father of one of my World War II army buddies. Lowry Bowman and I were two members of I Company, 397th Infantry, 100th Division, a very small group of men who had been through training, combat, and finally the post-war occupation of Germany.

As I reported earlier, it was during those demoralizing and tedious months of occupation that I became a Christian and subsequently experienced what I felt was a genuine call to the ministry. Shortly after my discharge, I hitchhiked from Chicago to Florida to see my old combat buddy. I spent two great weeks with him and his family, but I especially remember the evening at dinner when Lowry told his father that I was thinking of becoming a minister.

When Dr. Bowman did not immediately react, his son prompted him, "What do you think of that, Dad?"

Dr. Bowman turned to me, "Bruce, are you sure you want to go into the ministry?" "Well, it's either that or law," I replied, for I had been planning to be a lawyer since I was a child.

"Then I advise you to become a lawyer," Dr. Bowman said. "Only go into the ministry if there is absolutely nothing else you can do in life and be happy."

At the time I didn't know what to make of this reaction. Since my return to the States, I had been discussing my new plans with a lot of people. They were usually either awed by my piety or doubtful of my sanity. But I found the attention I received through both reactions very ego-satisfying.

Find God's Will before Worrying about the Cost

I've since come to appreciate Dr. Bowman's response as some of the best advice I ever received about discovering God's will for my life and considering the cost of the adventure with Christ. It put the matter of my call into a different perspective and made me sort out my own motives as I wrestled with God's will for me.

193

Did I really want *more than anything* to be an ordained minister?

Four years later in my first year of theological seminary, I met another man through whom God brought a life-changing insight about finding and following God's will. I had signed up for a Holy Week retreat at Schooley's Mountain, New Jersey, with one of the pioneer missionaries of our century. Dr. Samuel Zwemer, then in his eighties, was the first Christian missionary to go and live and work in the Moslem world. At that time the Moslems were so hostile to the Christian cause that no one had dared to attempt missionary work there. Nevertheless, Zwemer had gone off to the Arab world with his new bride, and for twenty years they did not make a single convert and they had no friends. They were outcasts for Jesus Christ.

A number of children were born to the Zwemers in this hostile land. But one by one most of them died of various diseases. Considered infidels by the Moslems, they were denied burial in the local cemetery. So Samuel Zwemer built their coffins with his own hands and buried them in his own backyard. Eventually, Zwemer's wife died and her handmade coffin was added to those in the backyard. Still he stayed, waiting for his first convert.

I will never forget the text Dr. Zwemer took during those days of the retreat—one he used over and over again: "Let no man trouble me for I bear in my body the marks of the Lord Jesus Christ." Of course these were the words of Paul who had suffered so much for the sake of the gospel. Zwemer was claiming those same credentials. He had paid a great price to follow what he thought was God's will for his life.

Both of these men left a mark on me. Both have helped me understand that finding and doing God's will for your life demands at the very least a single-minded dedication and in some cases a very great price. Through Dr. Bowman and Samuel Zwemer, God made it clear to me that the real model for a life of faith is one who has a single-minded obedience to the will of God, whatever the cost.

A Great Cloud of Witnesses

As we consider "committing it all" to God and his purposes in the world, we are not alone. We find models for this life of faith throughout the Scriptures.

I love that great chapter on faith in the Book of Hebrews, especially the words at the end. After describing most of the great heroes of faith, the writer concludes the eleventh chapter and begins the twelfth with these words:

"And what more shall I say? For time would fail me to tell of Gideon, Barak, Samson, Jephthah, of David and Samuel and the prophets—who through faith conquered kingdoms, enforced justice, received promises, stopped the mouths of lions, quenched raging fire, escaped the edge of the sword, won strength out of weakness, became mighty in war, put foreign armies to flight. Women received their dead by resurrection. Some were tortured, refusing to accept release, that they might rise again to a better life. Others suffered mocking and scourging, and even chains and imprisonment. They were stoned, they were sawn in two, they were killed with the sword; they went about in skins of sheep and goats, destitute, afflicted, ill-treated—of whom the world was not worthy—wandering over deserts and mountains, and in dens and caves of the earth.

. . . Therefore, since we are surrounded by so great a cloud of witnesses, let us also lay aside every weight, and sin which clings so closely, and let us run with perseverance the race that is set before us, looking to Jesus the pioneer and perfecter of our faith, who for the joy that was set before him endured the cross, despising the shame, and is seated at the right hand of the throne of God" (Heb. 11:32 12:2, RSV).

No, we are not alone.

History's Heroes of the Faith

This part of Scripture makes it clear that following the call of Jesus Christ involves some kind of personal cost. And the mighty acts of faith did not cease with the writing of the Book of Hebrews. Every age has had its models who have heard the authentic call and who are similarly running the race with perseverance, looking to Jesus.

Francis Xavier, one of the original band of Jesuits, is one such model. Francis Xavier was one of the richest and most privileged young men in Spain at the time of Columbus when Spain was the wealthiest and most powerful nation in the world. Francis lived in a splendid palace situated regally on the pine-clad slopes of the Pyrenees.

The first thirty-five years of his life were spent in romance and combat, chivalry and exotic adventure. In his thirty-sixth year he turned to the pursuit of knowledge and wisdom. He began to lecture in Paris and his brilliance confounded his peers. But standing in the back of the hall at almost every lecture was the young Ignatius Loyola, then a student and later founder of the Jesuit Order. At the conclusion of every lecture, Ignatius Loyola posed the same question, "But what shall it profit a man if he gains the whole world and lose his own soul?" Relentlessly Loyola attached himself to the brilliant young professor, asking the same question over and over until Xavier finally responded to the call of Christ. He became a monk and devoted his life to propagating the good news of God's love to all the world.

He set out first of all for India, where with eloquence, agony and tears, he shared the wondrous story of Jesus and his love. Twenty-one out of twenty-four hours, seven days a week were spent preaching the gospel and helping people. From India he went to Japan and from Japan to China. In the course of ten short years he learned to preach in twenty different languages. He traveled from place to place by begging passage on troop ships or sailing with pirates. On every ship he spent his time in the fo'c'sle with the crew trying to win them to an acceptance of and allegiance to Jesus Christ. Alone he crossed burning deserts and wound his way over snowy mountain ranges. He threw himself into the battle for the souls of men with the same vigor with which he had once approached military combat.

After ten strenuous years of ministry, Francis Xavier died at age forty-five, a spent, worn, emaciated man. Alone and untended, he quietly resigned his soul to God on a lonely beach in Siam. Those who found him reported that he died as he lived—with a smile on his face. No dour saint was he. His life was one long song sung to the glory of God. The poor heard him gladly and little children everywhere flocked to him.

Whenever I read about that "great cloud of witnesses" surrounding us as described in the Book of Hebrews, I invariably think of John Wesley, perhaps one of the most influential figures in English history. As I mentioned earlier, his preaching and the Methodist class meetings he founded changed the social structures of his time.

Wesley's influence was and is enormous throughout the Christian church. But John Wesley was never accepted in his own church, the Church of England. He lived and died an outcast of his own denomination—though to the end he considered himself an Anglican, never a Methodist. The price he paid for following God's will as he understood it was rejection by his own church.

To attempt to know and do God's will involves a cost for each of us and we rarely know in advance what that cost will actually be.

The Ultimate Model

Jesus' death on the cross was the ultimate price he paid for following God's will but it was not the only price. The mystery of the incarnation is that Jesus became human and paid a great price in *human* terms to follow God's will. First he had to accept his family's lack of understanding of him and his ministry. They were not only embarrassed by him, they actually thought he was crazy.

After his ministry began, he never had a home or a place of his own. He traveled about sleeping in a field, a cave, or a tent along the way. At best, he lived in somebody else's guest room. This last situation is one I can especially identify with. I traveled for many years for a faith mission whose funds at that time were practically nonexistent. Invariably, I traveled wherever free lodgings were provided. We could not afford hotel or motel rooms. I slept on sofas, in spare rooms, doubling up with young children, even on one occasion under a dining room table. For me, having to be away from home and giving up my privacy for borrowed lodgings was especially costly. But in my case I had a home to return to. I have a special respect for the people who, like our Lord, have no place that is "home" and who for the sake of the gospel are spiritual gypsies, living out their whole lives in other people's homes.

Jesus also paid the cost in human terms when he gave himself totally to twelve friends. One of them ultimately betrayed him and the others seldom understood him. We read that at one point he said to them, "Will you also go away from me?" Instead of denying or protesting, they said in substance, "Well, we would if we had some place to go." Paradoxically, he entrusted his world-changing ministry to a group of people who argued about which of them would be the most important person in the coming kingdom.

Jesus also paid the price of wondering whether he was doing God's will at all, a price exacted from anyone who is trying to know and do the will of God. Facing death at age thirty-three, he wrestled with God's will for him in the Garden of Gethsemane until great drops of blood stood out on his forehead. He went to the cross, having finally accepted God's will in the garden and yet again toward the end he cried out, "My God, my God, why hast thou forsaken me?" All of these experiences represent part of the cost paid by Jesus to do God's will. They are the kinds of things we may be faced with as well, as we see what the cost of discipleship could mean for us. To hear the call to adventure is to sign a blank contract accepting whatever the cost may be.

Present-day Heroes of the Faith

Another person I often think of in connection with that famous faith chapter in the Book of Hebrews is a man I met some years ago. Clarence Jordan, who has since died, was a brilliant theologian and Greek scholar who decided to take the Bible's injunctions literally. The Bible says that if you have two coats and your brother has none you give him a coat, and Clarence Jordan believed it. He started the experimental community of Koinonia in Americus, Georgia, and he shared whatever he had with the poor blacks in that community. His concern for the poor extended to housing, jobs, and developing agricultural know-how.

But Jordan did this at a time when the civil rights issue had scarcely been raised. His neighbors threatened his life, dynamited his house, shot at him and his family, and boycotted him economically. His experiences are right out of the eleventh chapter of Hebrews. Jordan's understanding of God's will for his life was simple. But there was nothing easy about doing it.

We invited Clarence Jordan to come to a conference in New York City a number of years ago, and I'll never forget his address on Saturday evening. He spoke with an authority few of us had ever heard or experienced. He was doing the will of God as literally and simply as he knew how and his words pierced every heart.

Another of my personal additions to the heroes of faith described in Hebrews would be my old friend, Corrie Ten Boom. She is now a famous best-selling author and is on television frequently, but I knew Corrie thirty years ago as a newly arrived Dutch immigrant. She and her family had been imprisoned under the Nazi regime in Holland for befriending Jews. The Nazis had ruthlessly killed her father and her sister. But Corrie Ten Boom found Jesus Christ in prison and set about to love her enemies and to forgive them and to win them for Jesus. She started a fire that is still burning. The will of God seemed simple for Corrie Ten Boom. She read that we are to love our enemies and to preach Jesus. But to do so in her case must have been immeasurably difficult.

While I was writing these words, an old friend and his wife came to our front door unannounced. I had not seen them in at least ten years. Some years ago Paul had heard God's call to adventure and he was prepared to pay the cost. With his wife and children's consent, he left a high paying job in the steel industry and began a new career in midlife as a teacher in a small boys' school in Connecticut. His salary was one-fourth his former salary and his housing was mean and cramped by comparison. But I never once heard Paul or his family complain. He was doing what he felt God wanted him to do—working with people on a one-to-one basis in small classes—and in spite of the difficulties he seemed to be hilariously happy. He is still happy and fulfilled, though he has now moved to work for a Christian youth organization at a modest salary. My friend Paul is certainly no hero in his own eyes. He is simply trying to serve God and help people.

A Call to Risky Living

Jesus gave us a strange paradox when he said, "He that would seek to save his life will lose it; but he that loses his life for my sake will find it." In other words, when we abandon our life to God's will in costly and sacrificial ways, we are not only building his kingdom, we are becoming everything that we are meant to be. We are called by God to this kind of risky living because in doing so we become fulfilled human beings.

Recently I read that every time Evel Knievel makes a spectacular leap across some obstacle or chasm, thousands of little boys and girls end up in our nation's hospitals the next day with broken arms and legs. They try to emulate Evel Knievel by leaping across ditches and culverts and jumping off roofs on their bicycles. Evel Knievel's awesome power over the young is not due to his winsomeness or maturity and certainly not to his judgment. But there is an Evel Knievel in each of us which this living model calls forth. When we see someone doing something extravagantly risky, many of us know down deep that this is how we would like to live. And I believe that each of us consciously or unconsciously is looking for a cause that we can join or a high prupose to which we can give our lives because we suspect intuitively that this is a large part of what life is all about.

We Are Not Alone When We Go Out to Risk

A friend of mine teaches first grade, and she told me this story about an incident in her class. At the end of a particularly long hard day she decided to scrap the lesson plan. Instead she had all the first graders sit in a circle and tell each other what they wanted to be when they grew up. One by one each child got up and announced, "I'd like to be a nurse like my mother," or "I want to be a banker like my father," or "I want to be a teacher like you, Miss Smith."

The last child to speak was the shyest and timidest little boy in the class. He said something like this, "Well, when I get big I'm going to be a lion tamer. I'm going to work in the circus. I'll get in a cage full of fierce lions and tigers with my gun and my whip and my chair and I'll make those animals leap through hoops of fire and obey all of my commands—" Suddenly, in the midst of this exciting tale, he looked around to find all of his classmates staring at him with their mouths open. He realized they were finding it hard to believe he of all people was going to be a lion tamer. Embarrassed, he was quick to reassure them. "Well, of course," he stammered, "I'll have my mother with me."

Let us take no one for granted. No matter how shy, cautious, ingrown, or introverted we may look, each of us in our inner recesses may be a potential lion tamer. And we will not be alone. When Jesus calls us, he does not promise us safety, long life, or even good health. But he says, "Lo, I will be with you always even to the end of the world."

Chapter Eleven

Into All the World

MEMORANDUM

TO: Bruce

FROM: Keith

RE: Chapter Eleven—Into All the World

Dear Bruce,

This one is really difficult in some ways. Since most Christians—including us professionals—have had almost no effective training or experience in changing organizations and institutions in the world, we feel like we are going out to hunt elephants with a BB gun.

But after what you and I have seen the past few years, I believe we are about to see more effective change in institutions through the efforts of Christians than at any time in history. I have the feeling we Christians sitting in the pews of churches across America leave the keys to an enormous amount of secular power in our glove compartments when we come to worship on Sundays.

But to begin with, how about discussing some of the questions we should ask in deciding where and how to help? Then, how can institutional change happen? How do we find a focus, set obtainable goals, decide on a strategy, marshal support and assess the opposition? Please give us some background information concerning how to assess our hopes, opportunities and chances of success regarding the instigation of institutional change.

Hope to see you and Hazel soon to get caught up. I'm sure glad we're friends!

Keith

There is a hospital in London which specializes in "terminal" cases. Only patients who have been diagnosed as incurable are admitted. But the atmosphere of this institution might surprise you.

You might expect this "place for the dying" to be dreary and depressing. Far from it. It is run by specialists in life, rather than death. They want life to be everything it possibly can be for those who have come to spend their remaining weeks, months, or years. Quite unexpectedly, some of the patients there have experienced a reversal of their terminal diagnosis.

This unusual medical facility is founded on the conviction that to be wholly alive you must in some way be spending yourself on someone else. Contrary to what happens in most other hospitals, no one is simply on the receiving end of medical attention, care, and concern. Each patient is assigned someone else as a daily project. For example, a person who is crippled might be assigned to write letters and read books for a blind patient. Someone who is blind can push a wheelchair for someone else who can see and issue directions.

I believe that this unique institution is operating on a Christian principle which is universally applicable. To be merely a consumer, not just of goods but even of love and concern, is deadly. It is psychological death. It is physical death. It is certainly spiritual death. To be spiritually alive we need to be investing ourselves in the wellbeing of our brothers and sisters. But no one can invest himself or herself in every cause. How do we decide if and when we should go beyond helping individuals and move into the institutional pain and lostness of our generation?

Examining the Options

As we think through our call to "go into all the world" it seems logical to examine the different possible things we might do to help. Not all are called to bring about large-scale "institutional change" as we usually think of it. The options are varied. Who are you to help? How many people at any given time and how? Of the numbers

203

of options available, God has one particular ministry for each one of us at any given time in our life. To find that option, to accept it, and to fling our life and resources after it is to be a neighbor to our neighbor, a brother to our brother, and a sister to our sister. It is also the means for finding life for ourselves.

Let's deal first of all with who we are to help or how many. It is possible that an entire life can be spent profitably helping just one other person. The most dramatic example that comes to mind is the educator of Helen Keller. Annie Sullivan's task was enormous—to reach and teach a blind, deaf and mute girl. The concern and dedication of Annie Sullivan produced one of the great luminous spirits of our time. But even had she been dealing with someone of more ordinary intellect and ability, she would probably have considered the investment worthwhile. This kind of one-to-one ministry through both professionals and amateurs is taking place all over the world at this very moment.

Perhaps your ministry is or will be to a group of people through some organization or program: taking on a scout troop, a class for slow learners, a ministry to prisoners, a visiting program for a nursing home. All around us there are groups crying out for love and caring and leadership.

Some people have chosen a profession which can be a means of reaching large numbers of people. One teacher I know has discovered a new way to relate to particular problems of childhood. This new friend of mine now teaches a regular workshop where hundreds of teachers in day-long seminars are learning some of her creative methods for unlocking the minds of small children.

Still others may be called to work for widespread social change. The last two decades have dramatically pointed up the effectiveness of this kind of serving. Many people have felt a call to work for civil rights and equal opportunities for blacks, women, and other suppressed groups.

Much rarer, but just as needful, are those people who have attempted a ministry to all of society. Ralph Nader is just one well-known example. The cars we drive, the planes in which we fly, the safety equipment which protects us—these are just a few of the areas of concern of this one man and his associates. He is a highly visible and effective consumer's advocate. On a less dramatic level, we occasionally read of stockholders in major banks and corporations who exert pressure to change what they consider to be immoral or enslaving practices in those organizations' investments or outreach.

Institutional Change: How Can It Happen?

All of these represent opportunities for ministry. But in this chapter I would like to explore specifically the politics of institutional change, something both sophisticated and difficult. Not everyone is called to involvement at this level. But some who are presently involved in a one-to-one ministry or a one-on-group ministry through their profession may eventually, as events change and skills are discovered, be involved in bringing about institutional change. If and when that happens, here are five considerations that may increase your chances of success and fulfillment.

Find Your Focus

First of all there is the matter of focus. Trust your own feelings in picking out your particular project. Believe that God has prepared you to minister in some specific area of human need. As Keith suggested in chapter 6, a clue may come through the kind of newspaper stories that grab and hold your attention, provoke your anger or sympathy. Another hint may come through the kind of people who seek you out to ask for help or share their problems. Do you find you continually bump into the same kind of problem situation? Out of the whole sea of human need believe that God wants to draw your attention to one particular area of concern. There may be no one else in your Christian group who shares your concern. In that case God may be calling you to work within a purely secular group where they are dealing with the pain or problem that has your interest. For instance, what can we do about shaping a more realistic and equitable welfare system?

Set Obtainable Goals

When you think you have found your particular project, decide prayerfully and with the counsel of others who have similar concerns specifically what you want to accomplish. This is the time for marshaling power—both God's power and your own special circle of human power and resources. Someone has said that power is the ability to move something from here to there despite apparent obstacles. To change things in the life and workings of an institution, you will need to marshal all the power and resources at your disposal and to isolate the specific things within a general area that you can accomplish. The narrowing of goals is essential to your success.

For example, I live near a large migrant settlement. It is the place where most of the winter vegetables are raised for the eastern part of the United States, and it draws a large migrant work force. This influx of largely uneducated, poverty-level people creates all sorts of needy situations. Many people of goodwill and of Christian conviction are trying to help in relevant ways. But there is, of course, no one approach to solving all the problems.

Some groups are concerned about the problem of housing. For other groups, wages are the issue. One approach is to try to influence the practices of the large corporations and businesses which control the lives of hundreds of migrant workers. Another group is actively engaged in organizing strikes and generally agitating to improve conditions for the transient workers. Another ministry is focused on the children of migrants—their education, their recreational opportunities, their health and welfare. All sorts of people of concern and goodwill are using their limited amounts of power to try and accomplish specific tasks to remedy a problem situation in one small Florida town. Each of these groups has zeroed in on a particular goal.

Decide on Strategy

But having set a specific goal, the next step is to decide on a strategy. Strategy is simply a logical progression of steps using whatever available power you have to "move something from here to there despite apparent obstacles." Sometimes the timing in a situation precludes a lengthy strategy. In the case of the migrant workers, a strike for higher wages must be called while the growing season is on, obviously, or the workers will have no more bargaining power until next year's harvest.

But for most situations where there is time to think through an effective strategy, the next step is to bring that strategy to bear at the right time and place. Any area where discontent exists may be a great place to start the process of creative change. Where discontent is openly felt and actively discussed there is usually a readiness for change. Sol Alinsky, the famous grass-roots organizer, used to say, "Rub the bruises sore!" In a different way, we Christians can bring about change by building on discontent, believing that this may be God's own opening wedge. For instance, Luther and the reformers brought about the Reformation by highlighting and building on the widespread disillusionment and discontent within the Roman Catholic church. John Wesley did the same, stepping into the political and spiritual vacuum of the established church in the England of his time.

Marshal Support

Another consideration in successfully bringing about institutional change is to assess realistically who is on your side.* To do this you will need all the wisdom and guidance you can muster. First of all, find out who are the shapers and makers of opinions in your particular area of concern. As Ed Dayton and Ted Engstrom say, "In every organization there will be those who, because of their position, or because of their personal influence, must be convinced of the need for change before it can be brought about. To attempt to steamroller new ideas past such people usually ends in disaster. The goal that you are trying to accomplish must be owned by someone who has the capability and the power to bring it about."[1] So, if you are attempting some large-scale project, pray and ask God to direct you to some of the opinion-makers in your area who might share your concern and whose support might be enlisted. In a church situation, for instance, our ideas for programs and strategies are often frustrated because we do not first enlist the support of influential church leaders or board members—not to mention the pastor. Unless some of these opinion-makers, sooner or later, are for you and for what you are attempting, you will almost certainly fail. If you succeed in enlisting powerful and forceful people in your cause, they may prove to be valuable resources in terms of leadership as well. One way to enlist the help of influential people if you do not know them personally is to see if you know someone who does. Then ask that mutual friend to arrange a meeting or an introduction. Of course, when you begin, you may have no one at this level with you and you may have to witness and work with a few ordinary people for a long time. But if your cause is right and you are willing to work long and hard at it, eventually you can go to people in power and some may hear you, and take the ball through the line and across the goal.

A friend has spent a good many years of his life trying to effect change for the inner-city poor in New York City. He told me that at the beginning of his ministry, he repeatedly made the mistake

---

* This comes after you have developed an "organic" group and committed your lives to God and his purposes in the world.

of assuming that all of the rich people he dealt with were his enemies, against any programs for helping the poor. He felt hostile toward the rich because he identified with the poor.

Now, we cannot deny that some of the rich (and that includes many people of means in the middle class) do intentionally or unintentionally oppress the poor. Nevertheless, many people of wealth have great concern for the poor and oppressed peoples of our country, and this concern can be harnessed to help. My friend eventually found some of his best allies in the rich and the powerful. In any work you are attempting, never assume that someone is an opponent until he or she proves to be one. Jesus said, "He who is not against you is with you." You need to enlist all the allies both official and unofficial that you can find.

But in marshaling forces to bring about change, don't stop with the obvious leaders and opinion-makers. There are all sorts of less obvious people of influence you will need on your side. I know an ambitious young man who started work with a large company with his eye on quick promotion and eventually a top job. The first day on the job he took a book that supplied pictures and short biographies of all the executives. He set out to succeed in that organization by knowing and winning support from the people in power. He read his book faithfully, memorizing the names and backgrounds of all the VIPs. But he said that after two weeks he realized his task was hopeless. A year and a half went by before he began to find out who the "important" people actually were.

For example, there was no picture or biography in his little book for someone named Gladys who proved to be the most important person in the organization. She was the executive vice president's private secretary. Her boss had so many key decisions to make every day that he relied on Gladys to suggest the most urgent ones. The only way to get quick action from this busy executive was to work through his secretary. If you won her support for your ideas, she had the power to promote them. My friend explained that he found a number of people like Gladys in the structure of the organization. They had enormous power to either facilitate or block any new programs or policies.

In every organization there are those people who are in obvious leadership roles—crucial to the success of any innovations. But don't overlook the less obvious people who may prove even more important. Recruiting the right people to promote your cause can be the most important single consideration in bringing about institutional change.

Assess the Opposition

But just as important to the success of bringing about organizational change is to know who is against you. Just as we are sometimes surprised to find some people on our side whom we had not expected to be, we are usually shocked to discover that some of the very people we assumed were allies are not in favor of our project at all. To be realistic about your opposition and to deal with it lovingly and firmly requires statesmanship. You cannot be naïve at this point and succeed. Remember that Jesus also said, "He who is not for you is against you."

In the town where I live there is a dreadful slum. Most of the shacks that line the road have no running water, no indoor toilets, and no screens in the windows. The poorest of the poor live with their families in these wretched buildings.

Many groups have tried to institute change in this area and build new housing. However, opposition comes from some strange quarters. It is not just from the landlords who own these buildings and collect their modest rents. It comes from housing authorities and county commissions and other groups whose "rights" and "privileges" are being threatened by proposed changes they *did not instigate*. While there may be agreement about spending tax money to improve this area, there is an ongoing conflict about what should be done and above all about who will make the decisions.

Then in another area of concern there is the familiar situation in which a group of new and zealous Christians decides to bring some well-known evangelist or special speaker into their town. They assume that every minister in town will be thrilled and will welcome anyone who can add more souls to the kingdom. This is often unrealistic, to say the least. Some ministers are theologically opposed to evangelism. Their view of the church precludes the necessity for a new birth in Christ. But even those ministers who believe in conversion may feel threatened by someone who may be having more success at bringing it about than they are.

Two centuries ago Samuel Johnson of London said, "Men need no other provocation to enmity than that they find themselves excelled." In attempting to bring about institutional change your opposition may come from those who have identical values and goals but who simply do not wish to be excelled or threatened in their own field. There is no way to bring about change without coming to grips with the reality of this fact of sin in human life. It is naïve to assume that everyone in a helping institution is primarily concerned with helping people. Many institutional leaders have only a partial commitment to eradicating a problem and a great deal invested in maintaining the status quo.

This has been the subject of some recent studies by the American Management Association. Whether the institution is religious, profit-oriented, educational, or social, much of the leader's time is spent in maintaining the organization. It is not surprising therefore that your ideas for projects requiring more work do not receive his immediate attention, interest, and cooperation.

We said earlier that we must never take people for granted. And those who are paid to do something that we are trying to do as volunteers may not always be the friends and allies their titles suggest. Actually they may be threatened by what we are attempting and unconsciously undercut our efforts. Those people who are unwittingly against you and your program may be out of a job if it succeeds.

But having said all of this, we affirm that institutional change can and does happen and usually because God calls one person— not a committee—and gives him or her a vision. Such a person recruits others who share the vision. Together they decide on a strategy and pray about that strategy. They look around to see the obvious and not so obvious people who might be enlisted in their cause and who can help to build the goals and carry out the objectives. They are also realistic about their opponents and take them seriously.

Jesus' public ministry lasted only three years and yet resulted ultimately in institutional change the like of which the world has not seen since. We think of it as a highly personal kind of ministry, much of it on a one-to-one basis with people like Zaccheus, Nicodemus, or the rich young ruler. Perhaps the bulk of his ministry was the time spent in a small group with the twelve disciples who were eventually responsible for the spreading of the gospel. Yet Jesus taught and healed in great crowds as well, using both the synagogue and the temple as a platform. The entire world is different because of Jesus Christ and his concern for both the redemption of individuals and for the ultimate redemption of all the world, including its institutions.

MEMORANDUM

TO: Keith

FROM: Bruce

RE: Chapter Eleven—Into All the World

Dear Keith,

As you'll see, I have talked in my part of this chapter primarily about how Christians can tackle the world and its problems on an institutional scale using all the smarts God can give us.

I know you got some powerful help in the business of creatively tackling problems on a city-wide scale from our old friends Bill Milliken and Harv Oostdyk. Why don't you relate that and also some specifics of how their method of "synergistic propinquity" is working in other places? (Incidentally, you'd better explain that phrase—it sounds awesome!)

Did I tell you on the phone that I bought a new red bicycle? It's great fun to try and log ten miles a day so that I can keep up with you joggers.

Bruce

For years I've avoided certain "social action" ventures. Intellectually I could realize the long range value of marching with banners, or making speeches to crowds or writing petitions to make institutions and society at large aware of different injustices and needs. But so much of what was done seemed so ineffectual toward actually *changing* things or helping meet the specific needs and alleviate the current pain of the people involved in the injustices. The resources of the helpers seemed to be so few and weak in the face of problems and needs apparently requiring massive amounts of money and power. There ought to be some way, I thought, to deal with the pain more specifically, a way which would involve me more personally and directly.

And as I have looked at us in the Christian community, we've appeared to be fragmented and floundering with regard to dealing with brokenness and lostness and solving the real problems of modern society. We seem to be like a great valley of dry bones (Ezek. 37:1–4)—dormant, waiting to be called together and to have life and passion breathed into us. But recently Bruce and I, as a part of those dry bones, have heard a call to come to life and be the people of God.

As we have looked at the fragmentation around us in the major institutions, we have wondered what people like us could ever do without the backing of money and power. What new principle or idea would allow us to make a difference in a world where the cost of loving and helping have often grown even faster than the cost of living (e.g., the costs of medical, educational, and social services)?

Then recently I heard again something I'd heard a hundred times, which I had never related to helping people in the world, that small passage in Paul's letter to the Ephesians: that God's purpose is at the right time to *gather together* into a unity, a oneness in Christ, all the separated and broken parts in the world! (Eph. 1:9). That must mean that he wants to bring life, healing, and unity to the separate dry and "broken bones" in the world as well as in the church.

Could that *mean* also that part of the purpose and strategy of

212

the passionate people of God is to bring together like dry bones various isolated helpers and helping ventures into some sort of creative and effective unity in Christ?—so God can breathe new life and strength into them? Not only do I think this is so, but while this book was only a plan, some Christians came to me with a dream of how it might be done.

Some Wounded Christians with a Dream

It was several years ago and I was living on a small island off the Gulf coast of Texas. The telephone rang one day.

"Hello, Keith, this is Bill."

It was a friend who had been working in the ghettos of the lower east side of New York City for ten years. Bill's voice sounded very tired as he asked if he and a friend might come and see me. They wanted to talk about something which had to do with their work. When Bill and Harv arrived, I don't think I've ever seen two more exhausted men. They weren't just physically tired, they were emotionally and spiritually spent. In the name of Christ they had started out to help people in hostile, teeming ghetto streets. The emotional cost they'd paid in ten years seemed enormous to me. They looked haggard. They and their families had had no privacy. Their apartments had been burglarized. Bill's storefront office had been bombed and his life was being threatened more and more frequently.

But out of the cauldron of their own pain and frustration these men had discovered a way to change things in and through the major institutions of America which not only made sense but which could be implemented by ordinary men and women in any Christian group.

They'd done a study of the area in which they worked and discovered that there was one social worker of some sort for every *seven* people of high school age in that enormously crowded area. That included teachers, policemen, public nurses, welfare workers, attorneys that worked for the city, and others. But over 90 percent of the young people were receiving *no* personal attention from these people. In other words, less than 10 percent of the people were getting virtually all of the help, while 90 percent were not being touched in any significant personal way.

The tragedy was that there was almost no coordination. Two social workers from different agencies might not realize they were working back-to-back in the same neighborhood. Neither of them had any way to contact the other kinds of workers who might be dealing with the same people and problems in that area. The difficulties and needs were so massive that most of the workers they talked to were discouraged, cynical, and doing their jobs mechanically without much enthusiasm at all. The high schools had a horrible problem in that many of the students didn't even attend. They either failed and dropped out or simply disappeared. The result of all this and a good many more problems was that the lives of both the helpers and the people needing help were becoming increasingly fragmented and depersonalized.

Bill and Harv began to realize that if they could get these workers in contact with each other to work as members of unofficial "teams," the combined help they could give would be increased enormously. For one thing, by working together and exchanging information they could all learn more about the people and obstacles they were facing. As they tried this, it began to work. Morale and enthusiasm improved, since the workers now found people with whom they could share the difficulties, the joys, and the ideas they had in trying to help people in that ghetto situation. Also they could get in touch with other agencies in the area much easier. For instance, teachers could get help from police or some legal agency or medical facility when they needed it for their people, because they would be in touch with someone personally in those various helping institutions on their "teams."

Bill, Harv, and I sat talking late into the night at the beach. As we were discussing the implications of taking people who are already working separately in an area and putting them together in some kind of cooperating personal group in creative new ways, I felt my heart begin to beat faster. Suddenly it began to dawn on me that this simple idea might be what Bruce and I had been looking for for years—a way that God could use to breathe life and effectiveness into the helping efforts of his passionate people. I saw that we Christians can begin to bring together all kinds of separated concern and power into an effective unity, like a laser-beam focused on real and massive social cancers around us in the world.

Reorganizing to Help—in the Church

I saw that in our church efforts to help hurting people in the community, we often form committees on the basis of who will come out to committee meetings. And many times the people who wind up in charge have no notion of what's really going on in the area of concern. But what if, for the purposes of helping, we divided the church into groups on the basis of *vocational involvement?* For instance, all the people in the medical and paramedical fields would be in one group. Often the nurses and hall attendants know more about what's actually going on in the hospitals than the doctors—with regard to some of the problems. But the doctors wield most of the power. The interchange of information and the prayerful consideration of medical problems of the poor in a city could mean the difference between life and death for hundreds of thousands of people over a few years, even if only a few churches were interested.

For example, a group of ministers, doctors, business people, and social workers in Atlanta realized that the medical delivery system was not understood by the people who might benefit from it. That is, the medical services actually available to the poor were not known or understood by the people who could have benefited from them. The group got a map and put on it all the hospitals and medical facilities where the people could get free or inexpensive help. Then they found that by advertising the availability of the services they could get the patients in faster and get medical services to people who had had none before.

And the amazing thing about these efforts is that they cost almost nothing, since the facilities and the salaries of the social agents and the ministers and doctors et al are *already being paid.* But by combining the workers and studying the whole situation amazing things are beginning to happen.

The people in the legal and paralegal vocations in a church could meet together to discuss the problems of crime and the laws of a local area. Many times a policeman or somebody who works in a jail could, in the context of a loving and committed Christian group, give a judge and local attorneys information they could never get about conditions in the local jail—or concerning the treatment of certain prisoners of different races and nationalities.

All the teachers and educators in a congregation could get together and begin to discuss what's actually going on in the schools, and what's needed. School board members might learn an enormous amount about the schools from Christian teachers in their smaller groups. Parents could learn and also contribute information concerning the real problems in the local educational system. And the authorities in the group could "hear" better because the atmosphere would be one of prayerfully trying to alleviate pain and lostness on God's adventure rather than merely "complaining."

These Christian adventure groups could become education centers, teaching the whole city what's happening. They could begin to exert power and influence through their contacts in the church and in the community in ways that no individual or group of interested (but uninformed) lay people could. It is striking, when looked at this way, how much power in the average local community is sitting in the pews on Sunday morning. But unless we Christians do this, society almost never provides *effective* and *safe* ways for the people to get to know each other and discuss the problems in a given vocation across the boss-worker separations. There's no way for doctors, for instance, to even talk to the hall attendants or the nurses seriously about what's happening in the hospital. There simply isn't time on the job. And even if there are occasions provided by the hospital, the threat of criticizing one's employers or superiors makes deeply honest interchange very difficult for the less powerful employees— who might have some of the best insights. But if the members of a congregation decided to commit themselves to God and each other and to find God's will for them in healing the pain and lostness in their own city, revolutionary changes could take place through the application of the principles of "creative nearness" we've been discussing.*

And if, for instance, a group of passionate adventurers got together and prayed about the medical care of their community for Christ's sake, God might give them some very creative and workable ways that haven't been thought of yet to increase the quality and extent of medical care. An internist friend of mine in Kerrville, Texas, caught this vision on his own several years ago. With the help of a few others he started a free clinic on Saturdays for people who couldn't otherwise get medical services, a problem that had hardly

---

* The social theory which has come out of Bill and Harv's work is called "synergistic propinquity." Experiments in ghetto high schools and neighborhoods in Atlanta, Indianapolis, New York, and other cities have been going on for several years. For further information on this approach to social problems write to Dr. Charles Palmgren, I.D.C., 465 Boulevard, S.E., Atlanta, Georgia, 30312. Dr. Palmgren has developed this theory and some of its implications in the manuscript for a forthcoming book. The development of the ideas presented here is the result of conversations with Charles Palmgren, Bill and Jean Milliken and Harv Oostdyk, out of whose work the ideas came.

been touched before that time. Another group started a free clinic in St. David's Church in Austin, Texas, for people who were not poor enough for free help but too poor to pay for private medical care—a large and almost forgotten group.

The theory is applicable to almost any area of need. Near Oak Ridge, Tennessee, a group of Christians made an agreement with the fire department that the dispatching operator would call a member of their group right after he sent the firemen off to a fire. They took turns being on call throughout the week. The Christian "on duty" would dress and go to the scene of the fire to see if there was anything his group might do for the people whose property was burned. Since there are increasing numbers of fires in certain areas, and since the machinery of some social agencies often simply can't move fast enough to alleviate the suffering at the time of the shock, many people can be helped substantially through this kind of cooperative caring by people who are already living and working in the area of need.

In a completely different vein, some Christians are getting together to help people and churches who own stock in major corporations learn how to exercise their voting rights to change conditions affected by corporate activities.

The principles of creative nearness will work in dozens of different situations; that we already know. And it's a very Christian kind of principle. Jesus said that when two or three are gathered in his name, he would be with them. I think that when two or three in the same vocational area are gathered together in the creative name of Christ to pray about, analyze, and work toward the healing of pain and lostness in any specific area of the world, the unifying and magnifying effect Bill and Harv discovered will begin to take place. In other words, these principles are built into the Christian gospel. And they are just being rediscovered through the painful experience of Christians trying to work with other people in the most complex and threatening kind of social work ever undertaken.

There are already some very simple and creative examples of people helping synergistically in "public" situations.

Some Grass-Roots Examples

In Austin, Texas, a few years ago, a minister named Richard McCabe, who was head of Catholic charities in that area, gave challenging talks to two groups in the same week. One was the Knights of Columbus and the other was the Masons—two traditionally separated groups. After his inflaming remarks about the unreality of their approach to charity in their city, both groups asked him what they might do that was practical.

Father McCabe had noticed that the large city hospital which handled all weekend emergency cases did not have the staff to care for relatives of the patients. Yet many of these people were from out of town and did not know anything about where they might find a place to sleep, something to eat, or some kind of care for their children. There was a real need for some sort of social services help to those uninjured crowding the waiting room. The city had resources, but the question was how a way could be found to get those resources together for the use of these people.

The Masons and Knights of Columbus took on the job together. They called their project "Austin Hospitality," and made it a Friday and Saturday night service to the emergency room of the city hospital. They put together a manual listing the nearest motels and all-night restaurants, together with additional services and cost breakdowns. Father McCabe feared the expenditures would get out of hand, so each group placed $100 in escrow to cover the cost of the operation. But the men and women involved got so interested in what they were doing that they never drew any of the money. Instead, they paid the expenses, mostly for cokes and phone calls, out of their own pockets and with funds their organizations already had for such things.

There were a lot of synergistic side effects from this project. The plan called for the Knights and the Masons to share duties on Friday and Saturday nights from 7:00 until 1:00 or 2:00 in the morning. The additional benefit came from the hours with little or no activity. The men on duty, traditionally at odds, were then compelled to talk to each other. The experience of sharing the same labor of love was disarming. The individuals quickly became aware that they were really brothers, and they could discuss other problems and the work in which they were engaged.

The manual they developed had most of the answers the volunteers needed.* "Check in with the staff, don the green jackets, move around in the waiting area." Their log book tells some amazing stories, not so much of the plight of the stranded travelers but of the response of the locals. Here are some quotations from that book.

---

* If interested in this sort of helping write The Rev. Richard McCabe, 4310 Small Drive, Austin, Texas, 78731.

December 31: Knopp & Robbins—combed glass out of the hair of children slightly injured in a car wreck. Drinking drivers: Called relatives for rides home. Rainy night makes for wrecks: Pretty girl badly scarred. Someone ought to do something about drunk drivers. Pregnant woman just made it. Cigars all around.

February 10: No action until 9:30. Knifing in a bar fight. Car wreck—no serious injuries. Coronary—helped widow with funeral arrangements. Doctors and nurses worked very hard to save man. Child scalded. Mother stayed with child in hospital. We took other two children to grandmother. Quiet night. McGuire and McGuire.

March 6: Family from Eagle Pass badly injured. We were all pressed into action with ambulance drivers, doctors, nurses, aides, bystanders. High speed on rain. Ran out to an Austin lady's house to turn off stove under supper. Cut hand. She came to emergency room and forgot stove. Hospital staff pleased with our fidelity to this job. Hanley and Peterson.

April 10: Took two little children home to my house. Mother and father will be kept overnight for observation—badly shaken up in auto accident. Wife delighted. Our kids are grown so we had room. 1 a.m.—two-car accident with multiple superficial injuries—much sewing up. Pregnant woman delivered at emergency room door. I helped doctor with delivery and took baby from his hands and rushed it upstairs. Suit needs cleaning. Dobban and Wilson.

Father Richard McCabe is one of the most creative men in America in bringing together the existing resources of a city to give inexpensive or "free" help to those who desperately need it. The above material was taken from the manuscript of a book he's writing with specific outlines of how to involve the people in one's own city who are already trying to help in specific areas. (It was he and his organization who delivered the deer meat from our small group's efforts through B. B. Voyles' idea described in chapter 6.)

He has designed and helped implement a striking low-cost housing venture in the Texas cities of Temple, Waco, and Amarillo, funded by private capital with permanent financing through FHA. But the amazing thing about this whole approach is that there are hundreds, thousands of people already stationed all over our cities and counties and neighborhoods who have desire and resources to help. They're invisible to us and to each other, for the most part. But if we in the church really got serious about wanting to be the passionate people of God, with a little effort we can begin to find out who is on the track of loving and helping the people we've been praying about. When a group of church folks investigates the problems of our own cities, we not only have immediate access to the difficulties and inside information relating to the institutions in question—through church members working in or with those institutions—but we often have access to the power people in them who can cause change to take place most easily. Such Christian groups, reaching out within our secular institutions after prayerful consideration, can help some remarkable changes to come about which will relieve much pain and lostness in the world. But in the process we may begin to see flesh and life come to the dry bones of our own faith and have a very exciting adventure with Christ and each other.

Chapter Twelve

And Now ... to Begin

MEMORANDUM

TO: Bruce

FROM: Keith

RE: Chapter Twelve—And Now . . . to Begin

Dear Bruce,

My whole life has been replaying itself before me the past few days. I remember so many times over the years wishing I knew "what to do to be God's person in the world." I have no idea how many other people have wrestled with the questions we're discussing regarding helping people. But I hope this book gets into the hands of some turned-on Christians who would like to try some creative experiments as they are moving beyond themselves into life.

When we first thought about writing this book, you pointed out three dimensions to the fullness of a Christian's experience, using a passage from Philippians as a text. How about sharing these dimensions while you tell us where you are as you're finishing the book? How would you sum up what you've been trying to say in your part of these chapters—about the rewards, the costs, and the priorities of following Christ out into his hurting world?

Bruce, it's really been fun doing this book with you. I've not only learned a lot from you, but my life is different because we did it. I have a feeling that this experience will lead to a whole new chapter in my life. And I can't wait to see what it is! Thank you!

Keith

Way back when Keith and I first envisioned these joint books and the related study courses we knew it was essential to include one that dealt with doing the will of God in the world. But we delayed starting it until this year, and I am beginning to see God's hand in the timing, because it could not have come at a better period in my life.

Over these past five years I have been involved in a research project. These have been the most exciting and rewarding years of my life to date. It has also been a very comfortable interlude. I have spoken very little publicly. Instead I've been spending time reading about (and traveling to interview) the leaders of various kinds of secular and spiritual ministries throughout the world. One of the reasons I became involved in this research project is because of the painful years which preceded it. A number of personal vocational relationships crashed around my ears a few years ago. My instinctive reaction was to withdraw, to be closely involved with my family and as few other people as possible, and to spend my time reading, writing, and researching.

I'm sure that was God's best plan for me at that time. Most of us have a rhythm in our lives or in our relationships, one which fluctuates between intense involvement in the world and a kind of withdrawal that takes place when close involvement becomes too painful.

But now I realize that my comfortable isolation, which was necessary for a time, may be coming to an end. The cycle begins again, and I feel prodded to find my place in the suffering of the world.

One of the central facts of our faith is that God reconciled the world to himself through the death of Jesus Christ on the cross. The cross is historical fact, the great and pivotal moment in human history. But the cross is also a way of life. Christ died that we might live, and by his death he showed us how to live. The cross represents costly love: God loving people who do not necessarily wish to be loved. This is how Jesus loved us, and he commands us

223

to love one another in the same way—if we want to find life in its joyful fullness as God designed it to be.

Three Dimensions of Christian Experience

In the third chapter of Philippians, Paul speaks of three distinct dimensions of the Christian life. "All I want is to *know Christ* and *experience the power of his resurrection;* to *share in his sufferings* and become like him in his death . . ." (v. 10).

These three dimensions might be compared to three concentric circles. The outer circle of "*knowing Christ*" is of course the largest and includes all those who have met Jesus Christ and who have a relationship with him beginning here and now that shall never end. This is very different from "being religious." But Paul implies that many of those in the larger circle are without power in their lives. Those in whom the Spirit lives and who are enabled to bless and heal and liberate others represent a smaller circle within the larger circle. This smaller group has discovered "the *power of his resurrection.*"

But within these two circles is the third and smallest circle. In this bullseye are those who know God in Christ and the power of his resurrection. But they are also those who in fact "*share in the fellowship of his suffering.*" In this book Keith and I have been exploring this experience of sharing the fellowship of Christ's sufferings.

Going Far Enough for the Fun

The first time I ever heard Sam Shoemaker preach I was a student in seminary. His sermon was entitled "Go Far Enough for the Fun." His premise was that many Christians have just enough Christianity to make them miserable. In Sam's terms, it is only as we are able to expend ourselves for others in the way that Christ cared for us that "the fun begins." An authentic faith in Jesus Christ will cost something, but it is also going to be fun.

Sometimes it's hard to imagine that serving in difficult and sacrificial ways could ever be fun. But I read all the time about people who are discovering this truth in simple, workable ways. Close to my home there is an institution for handicapped and retarded children called Sunland. In recent months they have begun what is called a Regional Foster Grandparent Program. Currently, eighty-six foster grandparents have been assigned to one hundred seventy-two clients with special or exceptional needs on a daily basis. In other words, each grandparent has two foster grandchildren.

The foster grandparents in the program must be at least sixty years old, in a low-income bracket, and in good health. There are no educational requirements. After a forty-hour orientation program, each grandparent works with two assigned children individually for at least two hours a day Monday through Friday. These children are often difficult to be with and may show little or no progress. But the grandparents commit to stay with them.

It is exciting to see that some of these so-called "hopeless" children are already showing improvement. But I am also excited about what is happening to the foster grandparents. One man, a shrimp fisherman for forty years, says he never had time for anything but shrimp during all those years. Now, at sixty-eight, he is, for the first time in his life, enjoying being with children. He says, "I won't trade the experience for anything. I really enjoy the program." One grandmother's comment seemed to sum up the feelings of a great many recruits in the program: "It sure is rewarding. I wouldn't take a million dollars for the experience I've had here." These older adults have shouldered a difficult, frustrating, and occasionally heartbreaking job, but, obviously, they have gone far enough for the fun.

Taking Up Your Cross

Years ago I preached a sermon entitled "Thorns and Crosses." In it, I was attempting to differentiate between the burdens we bear simply because we are alive in an imperfect world and those we bear because we choose to do so. Those burdens in the first category, I compared to thorns, similar to Paul's thorn in the flesh: an illness, circumstance, or handicap he endured but over which he had no control. These thorns can include anything from job loss, illness, or death of a loved one, to lesser afflictions like poor eyesight or baldness. But a cross is quite different. It is something we choose because we love God and care about his people. By choice alone we "take up our cross daily."

The saints among us, past and present, are those people who have the ability to care passionately about someone else—an individual or a group or an institution, and who then channel that passion into concrete actions. Such a course can lead to pain and suffering. It may not lead to success. But this is the level of faith Paul urges us to attain. This is how we are meant to live.

Keeping Your Eye on the Treasure

Recently, I met an old friend who had just been to an annual church meeting of the Waldensian Church in Uruguay, a country said by some to be one of the most repressive police states anywhere. The Waldensians are pre-Reformation Protestants who originated in northern Italy. The several hundred delegates who met in the small church in Uruguay were subjected to a great deal of government pressure. At the outset of the meeting, government representatives gave them a list of six so-called "undesirable" persons with instructions to exclude them from any official church leadership. With characteristic courage and independence, the Waldensians elected those very six to the highest offices in the denomination, and they are prepared to suffer the consequences.

But the highlight of the meeting was the sermon by the moderator. His text, from the thirteenth chapter of Matthew, was, "The kingdom of heaven is like treasure hidden in a field, which a man found and covered up; then in his joy he goes and sells all he has and buys that field" (v. 44, RSV).

He drew several conclusions from that text, the first being that finding the treasure came as a surprise. He pointed out that we can live days, weeks, and years of our lives before we come upon a treasure of such magnitude that our lives forever after are different. We must not expect to find that kind of treasure every day. But when we do, life will never be the same again.

The second lesson of the text was that the man sold everything he had to buy the field. That's the message of this book: the treasure, which we would define as the discovery of God's love for us in Jesus Christ, will ultimately be costly. To enter the "fellowship of Christ's sufferings" which Paul speaks of may cost us all we have.

But the final point of this Waldensian preacher's message is one that struck me as most applicable to all we've been saying here: the man in the parable bought the *whole* field, not just the treasure. This is true of most of the treasures of life. Most of us marry in the certainty that we have found a treasure, only to find that we have also acquired an awful lot of field. In trying to do the will of God in a specific way, we discover there is no pure cause, no pure church, and no pure people with whom we can ally ourselves. There are only people like us! To know and do the will of God right now in the world we will always be presented with a number of questionable options because we and others are imperfect.

But, convinced of the presence of the treasure, and for the sake of the treasure, I buy the whole field. Much of it may be rocky and unproductive and require backbreaking labor. I may become a part of an organization or start an organization that will ultimately become more field than treasure. That's okay. God's passionate people, no matter how impossible the field may seem right now, never lose sight of the treasure, nor the one who put it there for us to find . . . and give away.

MEMORANDUM

TO: Keith

FROM: Bruce

RE: Chapter Twelve—And Now . . . to Begin

Dear Keith,

When I finished the material on the last chapter I felt like I did when I turned in my final senior theme in college—now I'm going to have to quit writing about what I think and go out and try to **live** it!

What do you see as the most important things you have tried to say in these pages? And where are you personally on the adventure with Christ as we are finishing the book?

I feel so keenly as we wrap up this project that we are not the people we were when we started. I am really praying about whether or not God might want us to join forces and find a particular place and a specific group of people with whom we might start to put some of these ideas into practice.

Bruce

For years I secretly thought I could succeed in doing great things for God if I would only cut loose and go with him. But now I believe that committing oneself to Christ and his cause, though exciting, is also a very humbling thing. There is much failure and sometimes little success. But I am beginning to realize that it is better to throw myself into a cause that is important and ultimately to be victorious, even if I fail in the short run, than it is to hurl myself into a cause that may succeed in the present but is doomed to failure ultimately.

Henri Nouwen says a great thing about living by throwing ourselves into the fight:

> . . . I should be happy to be a part of the battle, independent of the question of victory. The battle is real, dangerous, and very crucial. You risk all you have: it is like fighting a bull in the bull ring. You will only know what victory is when you have been part of the battle. People who have tasted real victory are always very modest about it because they have seen the other side and know that there is little to brag about. The powers of darkness and the powers of light are too close to each other to offer the occasion for vain glory.[1]

I'd love to throw myself into the cause of helping people with Christ without caring what happens to me. But I do care, and I get my priorities confused with God's. And again and again I have put off beginning the adventure of "going out" for him.

I have used all kinds of excuses: "I don't understand the problems of the poor, the minority groups, the prisoners," or, "I've got a family to support and educate to whom I have a prior commitment." But in my heart I know that these are only rationalizations to keep from facing my fear of turning loose of the tight control I exercise over my time and my vocational projects.

And my excuse of ignorance of the political and material issues is not valid anyway. Because I am convinced that although we must deal with the social, political, and material realities of life to love the world, the ultimate gift we Christians have to give is the gift of meaning and purpose in and through the lostness and pain of life. We carry with us the gift of an eternal perspective that takes some of the sting out of the incompleteness and failure everyone experiences in the world. And *these* things I have known about for years. So I have no excuse.

As we have said in this book: if we Christians want to be the yeast or the salt of the earth, we can only do so by being carriers of the Spirit of God. For only he can go inside the lives of those who suffer, where we cannot get with our material help. If this is true, then the first step of becoming really effective lovers for Jesus Christ is a commitment or recommitment of our *own* lives to God, asking him to fill us with his Spirit. Then, I think somehow we have to believe that the world *can* be changed and that we as carriers of the Source of this benevolent disease of Christianity can help people "out there" to see a whole new way to live. We may feed the poor, we may visit the prisoners, we may change the structures of society, but until the world finds hope in a God that transcends all the tragedy of history, it seems to me that our helping will always be creating new pits of insatiable appetites and needs faster than we can fill them.

How Do We Begin?—How Do I Begin?

All this talk about commitment and what we might do to love people has made me restless. And I want to tell you where I've come because of working on this book.

When Bruce and I first envisioned this project, it seemed like a logical and necessary sequel to the two books we had already written together.* A great many evangelical writers in recent years have discussed the beginnings of the Christian life and the pietistic phase of learning to pray, read the Bible, and meet in small group fellowships. Not quite as many writers have gone on to discuss the personal issues one faces in the world almost immediately after becoming a Christian: money, power, sex, sickness, and death, etc. But very few modern evangelicals have gone on to write about the dynamics and the cost of loving and helping on the adventure with Christ. I have wondered why it is that some men and women have joyfully "gone to the lions," have made almost unbelievable sacrifices of time,

---

* *The Edge of Adventure* and *Living the Adventure*

money, health, social position, and even family ties in order to be God's people for others. It sounded heroic—but grim.

Last Sunday I heard a sermon in which the minister talked about the "sacrificial life." His face was grim and he pointed out that God was going to be with us when we "try to do it." But there was no happiness in the way he spoke about living a life for Jesus Christ that might involve sacrifice. I knew when I first considered writing my part of this book that the men and women called saints, who had given themselves to Christ and done remarkable things to help people, were in many basic ways no more unselfish than some of us. And when I began to examine their lives, I realized what we have written here: that the "sacrificial life" is really choosing one *pleasure* over another.

And in this writing I have remembered that my own happiest times have not been when all was secure, but rather when I was stretching to learn or to fulfill a task which called for more than I had to give—and I was trying to give it. I have been deeply confronted in ways I couldn't have imagined as I have written and reread these pages. And I realize as the book is about to come to an end that suddenly *I* am facing a new threat of change and a new commitment to Christ of my whole future—including all that has come to me since I've been a Christian. And the frightening thing is that I'm writing this in a book instead of whispering it to God in my closet. Let me tell you a little about how this adventure has unfolded.

A Strange Turning Point

Almost two years ago I was visiting Bruce and Hazel in Florida. We were talking about the possibility of doing this book. As usual, we talked night and day. Bruce and I walked the beaches, sailed, and talked while we were eating and into the early morning hours. We all prayed together and tried to examine where we were going and what we were going to do in the book. When the time came for me to leave, Bruce and I were still talking—all the way to the airport. So much in fact that we missed my plane. By this time we were totally exhausted with our talking but had made the basic decision to start writing. Now suddenly, we were about thirty miles from Bruce's home and had almost three hours to kill before the next plane. We decided we would go to a movie. But there was only one showing at that time in the afternoon. It was called *Goodbye, Norma Jean,* the story of Marilyn Monroe's going to Hollywood to become a movie star. Neither of us particularly wanted to see the movie, but we didn't have anything else to do and had talked ourselves out, so we went. The movie was the story of a very determined young woman who was pretty and sexy and wanted more than anything in the world to be a movie star. She didn't really like men, so it was especially poignant when she found that in order to make it as a star she was going to have to engage in various kinds of sexual activities with influential men in the movie world—many of whom repulsed her—who could help her on her way.

When Bruce and I got out of the movie we were both very serious. We sat in the car a few minutes thinking about the story we'd just seen. Then Bruce turned to me and said, "Keith, to bring people to Jesus Christ would you prostitute yourself and do what Marilyn Monroe did with those men she didn't even like?" I looked at him and shook my head, "No." He said, "Neither would I. But discounting the moral thing, do you know what that means? That means that her commitment to becoming a movie star was more than ours is to the cause of Jesus Christ." We talked about what kinds of prices people are willing to pay for their dreams, to fulfill what they see to be their destiny in the world. It really rocked us both to realize that we had a lot of reservations concerning the kinds of prices we would pay and the kind of "sacrificial life" we were really willing to live for Christ.

As we sat there I began to realize that through the pain of the last few years in my life—which had seemed enormous—God had been calling to me periodically to get some singleness of vision about loving other people and not to be so wrapped up in myself and my needs. Most of the time I'd been so concerned about surviving and getting through the days and nights that I'd only been able to hear God calling to me vaguely, as if from a great distance. There were times of near despair when I felt his touch and allowed the Holy Spirit to fill me with his hope. There were poignant moments when I was moved to tears and could hear God calling me on to his purposes. But in a day or two I would back off and go about my busyness again.

I was living a strange paradox. On one hand I was sometimes helping people, listening to them, and trying to do what I thought God wanted me to. But somehow I knew that I had lost the passion I'd once had about loving people for Christ's sake. The paradox is that I was still sincere. But I was also only going through the motions as if I *didn't* believe in what I was doing. But I *did* believe. It's just that something wonderful had slipped through my fingers. And now, sitting in front of the theater with Bruce, I heard God calling me in unmistakable language to a passionate commitment of my life, not only to Christ, but to his church and its cause in the world—and I was both thrilled and frightened.

To those of you who have only been Christians a little while, having made a serious commitment that you are sure is going to last forever, I realize what I am saying may not make much sense. I, too, made a "total commitment to Christ" years ago and have committed my life several times since to do specific things like: going to seminary, becoming director of a renewal center, and making certain commitments to write or say something I was afraid I'd be rejected for saying. But there with Bruce in front of the theater, God was calling me to commit my life to Jesus Christ and to the specific purpose of helping people experience his healing Person. I felt he wanted me to come out of my small self-serving Christianity, to approach the broken people in the world in their pain and lostness and to help them and tell them that there *really is hope,* there *really is meaning,* there *really is concrete help,* as well as spiritual help, as one begins to reorient his life in that of Jesus Christ and his people.

Bruce and I looked at each other. We both felt this call to commitment in that moment. And so we prayed together in the front seat of Bruce's car in the movie parking lot in Fort Myers, Florida. And we offered the next few years of our lives to try to tell the people of America about a compassionate God who is calling together a band, a family, of passionate people to find out how to live together and to love a world and a church which is terrified of pain, difficulty, and rejection, and which cannot see that in the church of Jesus Christ the only way to find one's life is somehow to lose it for him and for others.

We don't know where this commitment will lead us. But through the writing of this book I am beginning to see that God is calling me to pull up the tent pegs of my own personal and material securities. I believe he may be asking me, with some of his people, to begin in a new way to live out the drama of the passion of Jesus Christ.

Notes

Chapter 1
1. T. S. Eliot, "Little Gidding," IV, *Four Quartets* (New York: Harcourt, Brace, and World, 1943).

Chapter 3
1. Wm. McNamara, *The Art of Being Human* (New York: Doubleday) p. 15.
2. C. S. Lewis, *A Grief Observed* (New York: Seabury, 1963), p. 21.

Chapter 4
1. Portions of this chapter and the next have been adapted from *The Meaning and Mystery of Being Human* by Bruce Larson (Waco, Tex.: Word Books, 1978), pp. 68–74.

Chapter 5
1. Graph adapted from John Dollard and Neal E. Miller, *Personality and Psychotherapy: An Analysis in Terms of Learning, Thinking, and Culture* (New York: McGraw-Hill, 1950), p. 356. See also the discussion on pp. 352–68.

Chapter 9
1. Alfred North Whitehead, *The Adventure of Ideas* (New York: Macmillan, 1933), p. 26.

Chapter 10
1. Louis Fischer, *Ghandi* (New York: New American Library, 1971).
2. Oswald Chambers, *My Utmost for His Highest* (New York: Dodd, Mead & Co.), p. 210.
3. Dietrich Bonhoeffer, *The Cost of Discipleship* (New York: Macmillan, 1963), p. 32.

Chapter 11
1. Edward Dayton and Ted Engstrom, Christian Leadership Letter, March 1978.

Chapter 12
1. Henri Nouwen, *The Genesee Diary: Report from a Trappist Monastery* (New York: Doubleday, 1976), p. 54.